STIFFING THE WORKING CLASS

STIFFING THE
WORKING CLASS

WELCOME TO THIRD-WORLD AMERICA

Clyde Bradley

Algora Publishing
New York

Library of Congress Cataloging-in-Publication Data —

Bradley, Clyde, 1958-
  Stiffing the working class : welcome to third-world America / Clyde Bradley.
    p. cm.
  ISBN 978-0-87586-900-1 (soft cover: alk. paper)—ISBN 978-0-87586-901-8 (hard
cover: alk. paper)—ISBN 978-0-87586-902-5 (ebook) 1. Working class—United States—
History—21st century. 2. Work environment—United States. 3. Industrial safety—
United States. 4. Industrial relations—United States. I. Title.
  HD8072.5.B726 2012
  331.25'6—dc23
                        2012001675

Printed in the United States

TABLE OF CONTENTS

SECTION I. THOSE WERE THE DAYS

CHAPTER 1. THAT WAS THEN... THIS IS NOW

Even when the disinfectant in the air was strong enough to burn the eyes, the underlying stench it was intended to conceal was almost enough to make a person vomit. It was my least favorite place in the plant but, unfortunately, it was also the only direct path to maintenance supply.

The bare plywood walls were dreary and depressing. The floor was always damp and usually slippery. Cracks throughout the dingy and faded linoleum exposed damp plywood, adding the smell of mold and mildew to the other repulsive odors brewing in the dingy passageway. The homemade door, which was nothing more than a piece of warped plywood on hinges, never closed properly, allowing the heat and humidity of southern Georgia to seep into the non-air-conditioned corridor, adding yet another dreadful element to the already almost unbearable conditions.

This was a disgrace I would never have dreamed existed anywhere in 21st-century America, not to mention in a food manufacturing facility. This was a disgrace that could easily qualify as the oxymoron of all oxymorons: a makeshift so-called "restroom facility" that was nothing more than a homemade plywood shanty elevated on 4 x 4 stilts and squeezed onto the side of the building, next to the trash compacter, that housed an almost endless row of odor-producing portable toilets—or to put it in proper oxymoron context, indoor outhouses.

This demoralizing excuse for a "restroom" was used by employees in the outdated "old facility." I was fortunate enough to be assigned to the brand new cook facility next door. So I only had to walk through this repulsive place when I needed something from maintenance supply. But even though we had luxuries like real, flushable toilets in the cook plant, it was a far cry from the State of the Art, World Class facility the company had advertised in their help-wanted ad.

More despicable even than the indoor outhouses was the lack of regard for safety issues throughout the entire three-building complex. Perhaps the worst example of unsafe conditions in the brand new cook facility was a CO_2 tunnel freezer. The maintenance staff received far less than the in-depth training that should be required before servicing a piece of equipment like a freezer where improper operation or malfunctions could be fatal. And we had operators we could not communicate with because they only spoke Spanish. They received absolutely no training on this equipment and would go behind us pushing buttons and changing settings with no rhyme or reason.

When the exhaust system's performance on this unit became compromised due to ice accumulating in the exhaust vents, the entire floor of the packaging area was covered with CO_2 fog, which causes breathing difficulty, followed by unconsciousness and eventually death if exposure continues.

Due to our limited training with this equipment, no one in the maintenance department had an immediate solution to the exhaust system problem. But that was okay — our "get the job done at any cost" management staff had a solution. They instructed us all to keep aware of our mental states and leave the area to get some fresh air anytime any of us started feeling dizzy or light-headed, or had difficulty breathing.

So for months on end, whenever we turned on the CO_2 freezer and potentially fatal CO_2 fog began slithering across the floor, people would take turns running in and out of the room to minimize exposure while management concentrated on more pressing issues like making the line run faster, reducing waste and eliminating downtime. All legitimate business concerns, for the record. But not legitimate enough to override safety.

It seems common sense would dictate that if you have potentially fatal CO_2 fog seeping into the atmosphere in a room full of employees, a room that was equipped with a CO_2 monitor that was known to be defective, no less, then that equipment should be taken out of service until the problem is corrected. But common sense was not held in high regard at this company. Things like safety regulations were seen as ugly hindrances, an extra cost factor, something that slowed down production and added nothing to the bottom line.

I'm not sure exactly what I was expecting when I packed up my family and headed to rural Georgia to take a position with a brand new cook facility in the poultry industry in an attempt to escape the low-paying Myrtle Beach job market. But this wasn't it.

I actually came into this business with high expectations. These expectations even included the possibility of staying on until retirement. I left four grown children and three grandchildren behind in a place I liked living, and moved hundreds of miles away to a place where I knew no one, to take this job. Not to mention dragging my wife and one remaining child under 18 with me. I didn't do that lightly. When I asked my family to make that kind of sacrifice, I was committed to be in it for the long haul and I signed on with considerable enthusiasm.

And why not? I was going to work in a brand new, State of the Art, World Class cook facility. And I was getting in on the ground floor as a member of the original maintenance crew. I had 22 years of previous experience in food manufacturing, including six years in production supervision that would, no doubt, be invaluable. As I saw it, there was nowhere for me to go with this company but up.

Of course, not all my expectations were positive. Working in poultry processing, I expected to be extremely cold. Or extremely hot, depending on what stage of the process I was involved in. I knew neither extreme would provide a comfortable working environment. I also realized that working around raw meat would be less than appealing. So in addition to temperature extremes, I was prepared for blood, guts and foul odors as well. And I knew being involved with the start-up of a brand new facility would bring a whole host of stressful situations.

But I didn't expect to work in a hostile environment where I was screamed at, threatened, intimidated and scolded like a child—many times with an extra dash of profanity-laced insults just for good measure—on a daily basis. I didn't anticipate two, three, sometimes as many as four or five managers standing over my shoulder every time I made a simple adjustment or repair, asking questions, getting in my way, and telling me I was working too slowly while their mere presence was usually impeding my progress. I didn't expect to have to operate equipment for so-called operators who didn't have a clue how to actually do their job and couldn't understand a word I said when I tried to help them because they didn't understand English. I never dreamed I'd be expected to work 14, 15, sometimes as long as 19 hours a day, for days and sometimes even weeks on end, with no notice, no thank you, and then be expected to be back at 6:00 the next morning. I certainly didn't think I would be expected to work in 480-volt industrial electrical panels when my resume clearly showed my maintenance experience was primarily mechanical with some experience in computer repair and low voltage electronics. And I didn't expect to constantly work in unsafe conditions with faulty equipment, be subjected to working in areas with irritating chemicals over applied by unqualified sanitation workers, and be exposed to Tuberculosis. But I got all of that and more.

I found myself dreading getting out of bed in the morning. I was working in America, yet somehow it seemed like I was magically transported on a daily basis to some third-world nation where OSHA standards and labor laws didn't exist. I felt trapped in a manufacturing environment that was slowly sucking the lifeblood right out of me. I hated manufacturing and I wanted out.

But it wasn't always that way. There was a time when I was actually proud to be a career American factory worker. But that was in a time and place that seemed like it was a whole world away—when in actuality, it may not have been a world away, just a couple of decades away. And a couple of decades made all the difference in the world in this modern manufacturing era of cost cuts and cheap labor.

My story begins over 30 years ago when I graduated from high school in a sleepy little suburb of Chicago, back in the summer of '76. Not being the higher education type, I opted to skip college and jump straight into the workforce. I didn't know exactly what I wanted to do in life, but I knew I wanted to do it without spending another four years (or another minute, for that fact) in school. Having seen family members dating back to my grandfather, as well as many neighbors, lead a comfortable life working in factories, that's where I focused my search. After a summer full of interviews, I finally landed an entry level job with a very large and successful food manufacturer, thanks to the help of a family friend's recommendation.

The work was far from exciting. My first assignment was stacking cases on the end of a line and it made for a long, boring day. But it paid well for what it was. Five bucks an hour to start with a 25¢ increase after 60 days. That was big money back in 1976, over double the $2.30 per hour minimum wage. Within a few months I became a utility man. This position allowed me to rove around the department freely, stocking lines with supplies, as opposed to being stuck in one spot stacking cases and watching the clock all day. It also increased my hourly wage by an additional 25¢ an hour.

Weeks turned to months and months quickly turned to years. My vacation grew from one week a year to two, then three, four and eventually five. As my seniority grew, so did my opportunities to obtain more prestigious and higher paying positions. I spent a little time in sanitation as a machine cleaner before heading to the second floor as a mixer. I also put in some time on a forklift before eventually becoming a machine operator, then a line tender, which was essentially a machine operator who was also responsible for making mechanical repairs, and finally a team leader. I was up to $8.00 per hour within a couple of years, over $10.00 before I knew it, and ended up topping out at a little over $19.00. Eventually, I even abandoned my "no time for college" philosophy and benefited from a couple years of higher education compliments of the company's educational assistance program, which, at least in part, helped me to secure my eventual team leader position. I never really intended to become a career factory worker. But by the same token, I never really intended not to either.

Once settled in, I realized this wasn't such a bad place to be. Obviously, I was never going to become wealthy in this occupation. But the pay was certainly livable. And the fact that the job also offered full benefits was invaluable as well, because once I turned 18 and decided not to attend college, I was no longer eligible to remain on my parents' health insurance.

And as I started to take further notice, I realized I wasn't alone in my career choice. There were countless employees at that plant that had 20 and even 30-something years of their lives invested there. And they were quite comfortable. After all those years of being paid livable wages, and thanks in part to various savings and investment plans offered as part of the company's overall benefits package, many were able to afford large boats, luxurious campers, and even permanent summer homes. And the majority of the workforce in that facility showed their appreciation for those luxuries back to the company in the form of hard work, commitment and dedication. There were a small handful of bad apples, of course, as there are everywhere, that would constantly complain or try to take advantage of the company's sometimes too lenient disciplinary policies. But the majority of the employees believed deeply in the age-old motto, "don't bite the hand that feeds you." And we were not only fed, but fed well.

So all in all, life was good for those of us fortunate enough to work on those factory floors. It was so good, as a matter of fact, that the facility rarely did any hiring. It was more commonplace for a position to become open due to a retirement or death than from a resignation. So the only time hiring became necessary was when a new product line was coming out and expanding the facilities production. And when that happened, hiring was done exclusively through referrals from current employees.

The company had such a good reputation as an employer, one time the word was leaked out through a local radio station that the plant was going to be hiring approximately 200 people to staff a new department and thousands of hopeful jobseekers showed up on a single day looking for applications. The entire neighborhood was in total gridlock from all the traffic. People were parking as far as a mile or more away from the plant—in alleys, private drives, in front of fire hydrants, anywhere they could squeeze in. Once parked and at the plant the aspiring candidates then had to brave a double line which stretched out for several city blocks. The vast majority had to be turned away as the plant simply didn't have that many applications to distribute, not to mention the manpower to review them. Some of the job seekers that were turned away empty-handed actually left in tears. The episode even made the Chicago evening news.

These were not glamorous jobs. The work was very repetitive. This was a facility that produced powdered drink mixes, dry package salad dressing mixes, barbeque sauce, pancake syrup and other products. The departments that weren't dusty were sticky. The ones that didn't smell fruity reeked of herbs and spices, pepper or vinegar powder. People went home at the end of the day wearing and/or smelling like fruit punch, garlic, barbeque sauce, or pancake syrup, or with their hands stained red from a long day in the powdered drink mix department.

Yet when the word got out that the plant was hiring, prospective employees showed up in masses. The plant adhered to a concept that, unfortunately, seems to have been long since abandoned by most American manufacturing facilities. Pay people a fair day's wage for a fair day's work, provide them with adequate benefits, treat them with respect, provide a safe work environment, make employee morale a top priority, and people will want to work for you. Not only will they want to work for you, they will want to make a long-term commitment to you.

I just shake my head in disbelief every time I hear employers try to justify hiring illegal immigrants by claiming Americans don't want the jobs they're offering. It's not the jobs Americans don't want. If Americans don't want to take jobs with particular companies or in specific industries, it's due to either insufficient wages, inadequate benefits, undesirable or unsafe working conditions, unfair labor practices—and in many cases, a combination of all of the above.

Chapter 2. Everyone Wants to Play on a Winning Team

Everyone wants to play for a winning team. And team building is every bit as important, perhaps even more so, on the work room floor as it is on the football field, basketball court or baseball diamond. It's a simple enough concept but, unfortunately, one that doesn't always translate well into the 21st century business world of reduced costs and cheap labor.

If you want to be the best, hire the best. If you want maximum output from your employees, put maximum input into them. If you want the same dependable employees to continue to show up and be productive every day, give them reason to continue to show up and produce. To borrow another timeless expression, sometimes you really do get exactly what you pay for—and not one iota more.

That dusty manufacturing plant I worked in from the mid-1970s through the late-1990s got it. They were a winner in every way. I'm not claiming the place was manufacturing Utopia. It had its fair share of problems. But through above average wages and benefits, fair workplace practices and a sincere concern for employee morale, this facility built an experienced and stable workforce that could rival any other workforce in the city of Chicago, bar none.

A production manager once told us collectively at a large employee meeting that our plant was almost always one of the first to be considered for new product lines because of our high quality rating, excellent safety record and most importantly, our flexibility and adaptability.

"This group can stop and turn on a dime," the manager proudly proclaimed to us. Our plant manager also told us on numerous occasions that we were often used as a corporate model for plant cleanliness. There was a constant barrage of visitors from other facilities around the corporation always strolling through the plant. And many times they were there for no other reason except "to see what a really clean plant looks like," according to our plant manager.

Constantly hearing statements like these made me proud to be part of that manufacturing team. They also served to strengthen my already sound sense of job security. But these things didn't just happen by mere coincidence. They were the product of decades of team building through training, trial and error and a genuine commitment to employee satisfaction.

This particular plant was non-union. And the company liked it that way. But again, they didn't just keep the union out by wishing it away. Nor did they stoop to threats or intimidation towards employees that may be leaning the union's way. They kept the plant in a non-union state by operating under the same guidelines as if it were a union plant. This was yet another example of a simple but effective method the company used to keep control of the big picture by exercising a little give and take in a smaller one.

That's not to say there were never union drives conducted at the plant. The unions would show up from time to time to pass out their literature and promote their promises of a better life through union membership. And they would gather a small cult following of employees that would clamor for change and attempt to rally the troops. But by already offering the same basic benefits that are associated with union membership, the company effectively removed any reason for most employees to vote for a union, and the membership drive would always go down in flames.

One example of company policy geared towards union policies was the plant's job bidding system. It was basic and simple but effective. Anytime a department had a job opening, it was put up for bid. Entry level jobs were easy. The most senior bidder was awarded the job. Higher level jobs were a little more complicated. They were awarded to the most senior qualified bidder, that is, the most senior bidder that had previously completed an on-the-job training program for the position. If no qualified bidders existed, the most senior bidder would enter the position on an on-the-job training basis and get the opportunity to eventually become qualified for that position.

Entry level bidding could be a very powerful tool. Most of the supervisors were reasonable, but if you were to find yourself dealing with one with whom you just couldn't see eye to eye, getting him off your back was merely a pen stroke away. And the OJT jobs brought a whole new element of opportunity—not only to make more money, but to build an extensive background in manufacturing operations from processing and operations all the way to maintenance. For a gung-ho youngster like I was back then, the sky was the limit. I would enjoy the luxury of first shift for awhile; then, when money was tight or I was tired of dragging out of bed at 6:00 AM, I would bid on a higher paying job on second or third shift, preferably one I was not yet qualified for, growing my qualifications list by leaps and bounds. And I also knew as I was gaining qualifications on the off shifts that eventually my seniority would be able to allow me to win job bids for the higher paying and more prestigious processing and operating jobs on first shift.

But perhaps even more unusual (for a non-union plant) than the job bidding program was the plant's grievance procedure. Anyone in the workforce could file a grievance for a variety of reasons. A grievance could be lodged against a particular management figure, if employees felt they were being treated unfairly, or they could challenge a company policy on the grounds of fairness, safety or employee morale. The procedure consisted of four levels, starting with the employees meeting with their supervisor to discuss the issue, and eventually allowing them to bring up their concern face to face with the plant manager and personnel director, if necessary.

Very few grievances made it to the fourth level. Most were settled in the first or second steps, with a simple meeting between the employee and a supervisor or a department head. The majority were also settled with a high rate of employee satisfaction. Yes, this was a company that held employee morale and satisfaction in high regard. And the results of these efforts were reflected in the overwhelming majority of new hires becoming loyal employees for 10, 20 and even 30-plus years.

Other tools utilized to keep a stable and motivated workforce included extensive training, emphasis on safety and comfortable working conditions, adequate facilities such as locker rooms with shower facilities, clean restrooms within a reasonable distance from all working areas, a medical department staffed with a fulltime nurse and a modern full service cafeteria with good food at reasonable prices.

Employee involvement was another area the plant strived to keep at high levels. No one was forced into any type of involvement above and beyond the responsibilities of the daily job. But those who were interested in going above and beyond could find opportunities in many areas. Early on, there was a cafeteria committee that employees could join if they wanted to have a say in the way the cafeteria was operated. Later years saw the creation of an employee-written newsletter where I honed my writing skills.

But without a doubt the one volunteer employee committee that stood above all others was the recreation committee. In addition to organizing an annual Christmas party and company picnic, they sponsored several outings throughout the year with discounted group rates for employees and their families and friends, to everything from professional baseball games and the Ice Capades to river boat gambling and other less traditional trips. The committee also sponsored a company bowling league for many years.

Not everyone participated in these after-work events. A few viewed them as a waste of the company's time and felt the money spent by the company to subsidize this committee and their events could have been better spent in areas that would benefit all employees. But the majority of employees participated in at least one or more of these after-work activities and they were wildly popular. And there was an even deeper benefit associated with the "invite family and friends" aspect that the company may or may not have been aware of. When the same people work together day after day for years (and many times decades), a sense of extended family bonding automatically occurs. Then when those extended families all come together in one place with their real families, the bonds grow even stronger.

Yet another area of emphasis at this facility was the importance the plant put on open communication. Bulletin boards were available in every department as well as in hallways, office areas and cafeteria, and they were updated constantly. Regularly scheduled employee meetings were also conducted in every department and the plant manager assembled his entire staff and met with employees from all departments four times a year for plant-wide quarterly meetings. These meetings would usually last an hour or more and cover everything from plant performance, safety, future scheduling, possible product line additions and subtractions, policy changes, and employee morale and it was all discussed in an open and honest atmosphere with the last part of the meeting reserved for no-holds-barred question and answer session between hourly employees and the upper management staff.

Perhaps the most effective tool used by management to promote employee satisfaction, however, was their annual local wage survey. The company would evaluate not only the wages offered by several manufacturers of similar size and type in the local area, but their benefits packages as well. The goal was not necessarily to be on the top of the pile on every category, but the plant strived to be in the above-average column on all fronts, giving their employees no logical reason to want to go work for a competitor. And in this goal they were highly successful.

CHAPTER 3. THE BEGINNING OF THE END

Eventually our large corporation was taken over by an even larger corporation. Extensive restructuring took place over the years, in the upper echelon of corporate management, but for the most part things remained the same at our local level. Years later, this growing conglomerate acquired another large food corporation. These two former companies were operated as separate entities initially, but eventually they were merged into one. There was obvious concern in our camp, initially, because although our new sister corporation was also an outstanding company to work for, their wages and benefits, on average, were slightly lower than those of most of our plants. At first this did not affect us, but slowly our happy little plant started feeling the repercussions of being slightly better off than the others. Our insurance benefits, although still adequate, began to get watered down. The sixth week of vacation offered to the 30-year veterans, of which we had more than the average company, was abolished to match the other company's five-week vacation maximum.

During this "concessions" stage, as our plant attempted to remain cost-competitive within the newly structured corporation, excess capacity was evaluated at all plants. Product lines were then shifted from one plant to another, paving the way to start closing plants to lower overall operating costs corporation wide. At first, product shifts meant that the new company's products were shifted among their plants and our products were shifted among our plants. However, once the decision was made that we were now one big, happy family and products were interchangeable regardless of their original origin, many of our original plants found themselves at a distinct disadvantage.

Our wages eventually became a target, and that, at least for me, became the beginning of the end. We also had a new plant manager. He quickly unveiled a plan to reduce workforce wages by six percent over a two-year span to make our average wage base more competitive throughout the corporation. Being a non-union plant, this plan could have just been crammed down our throats. But in the employee satisfaction driven, old-school fashion that we were used to, our plant manager brought the proposal to the workforce and asked for our support.

The major flaw with this plan was that it applied to the hourly workforce only. The higher paid salaried management staff was not asked to participate. The majority of the workforce supported the plan half-heartedly because we felt it might be the only way to avert a future closing of the plant. Most of us had invested decades of our lives in that plant and knew no other life. But this set up a "them" against "us" attitude between the hourly work force and management. I had never experienced that before.

This rift between management and production was extremely difficult for me to navigate in my new team leader position. I was considered a supervisor by the members of my crew. And with just cause, because the newly-defined team leader position combined the previous duties of the lead person and supervisor positions into one, all-encompassing role of floor support and office administrator. But unlike the supervisors of old, the newly-created team leader position was an hourly position. So although I was seen exclusively as a "them" by the members of my crew, I was undoubtedly an "us" on this issue. Thus upper management expected me, as a "management figure," to show my crew full support for this wage reduction. But I was every bit as angry as the rest of my crew. (A few of them actually refused to believe me when they complained about the wage reduction, and I told them I was taking the same pay cut they were.) Summed up in a nutshell, our plant manager, along with most of his staff, were saying that they were worth their compensation, in the eyes of the corporation, but we were not.

During the first year the wage reduction was in effect, attitudes on the workroom floor were just a little bit more on edge than I ever remembered them being before. Before the second annual three percent wage cut could take place, however, the company conducted a corporation-wide employee satisfaction survey, and based on the results the second phase of the wage reduction was cancelled. Apparently, in an anonymous survey the hourly workforce was not nearly as supportive of this wage reduction as upper management seemed to feel they were based on private, one-on-one, meetings between employees and management staffers.

Another cost-saving technique employed around this same time was the use of temporary employees. They could hire the best available workers due to the reputation this plant had built over the years by paying competitively, offering great benefits, emphasizing safety, and treating employees fairly; but the plant opted to stop hiring permanent employees and to depend instead on temporary employees hired through a staffing agency to fill entry level positions.

So we became a two-class working society. The permanent employees were well compensated, had great benefits, job security, a grievance procedure and a vested interest in the success of the plant; and the temporaries were paid a little over minimum wage, had no benefits, no job security, no grievance procedure, and had absolutely no vested interest in the success of the plant.

Temporary labor was not a completely new concept for this plant. We had been using day laborers for years. But their use was very specific. They were called when unexpected circumstances occurred, like when an automatic case stacking machine went down and there was not enough available manpower to do the job manually. Or occasionally when 100-pound bags of raw ingredients arrived in bulk and needed to be hand-stacked on pallets before being warehoused. For this, temporary labor worked fine.

But now, for the first time, we had temporary labor manning many of the packaging lines and serving as the final inspector of our quality before the product was packaged and shipped. And this wasn't necessarily a good thing.

One afternoon I reported to work and my boss was waiting to inform me that QC had performed a pallet audit on a pallet run on my shift and discovered an astronomical increase in defects. The last audit had been conducted before my department was overrun by temporary employees. If I remember correctly, the increase in defects since then was somewhere around 1800 percent. Apparently, my boss was expecting a panicked reaction from me; he was not amused when I responded, "I would have expected it to be higher than that."

It wasn't that I didn't care. Quite to the contrary. I cared so much that it was driving me crazy. But there was only so much I could do.

In fact I had been campaigning for months, to anyone I could get to listen, saying that we needed to be more concerned about the negative effect this endless revolving door of temporary employees could have on quality. Long before the results of this audit were made public, I had been conducting my own self-audits. I would pull random displays off the finished product line and visually inspect every single package in it. When I discovered a defect, I would take it back to the machine it was run on, show it to the responsible packer, and explain that they could not allow such defects to pass, on their way to a customer.

When I found myself returning to the same machines often (which was rarely the case when I had permanent employees manning the lines), I would sit down with those particular packers, inform them that they were not adequately identifying and removing defects, and ask them if there was anything they felt I could do to help them improve in this area. I was always careful during these somewhat awkward, impromptu meetings to emphasize that this was about searching for ways to build up the struggling employees and help them improve, not belittle them and tear them down.

Hand packing was not an easy job. On a perfect day and under perfect conditions, it might seem simple: pick up 12 pre-counted pouches out of a moving bucket conveyor in each hand, place one in front of the other into a display, repeat this step three times and then push the filled display onto a moving conveyor belt and begin the process over again. But perfect days were few and far between. Many times the pouches would lie less than perfectly flat in the buckets and would require considerable rearranging once they were lifted out, before they would fit in the display properly. Defects were not always at the top of the pouch stack and sometimes the packer had to fumble through the stack to remove them. Sometimes the bucket would not have the required 12 pouches and the packer would either have to add or subtract pouches before putting them into the display. On occasion, the displays would not open squarely, so the packer had to reform the display, while other times the automatic box-maker would skip or jam, forcing the packer to make displays by hand while trying to keep up with the pace of the line until the operator could tend to the situation. When the overhead conveyor system that transported the full displays to the packaging area went down, the packer would be required to stack the full displays on a cart until the conveyors started moving again. And many times, two or more of these situations would occur simultaneously.

These sometimes stressful circumstances required a cool head and steady hand to get through the shift. I had witnessed many experienced and dedicated packers hit their breaking points on problem-filled days. So I knew that taking people off the street, perhaps with no previous manufacturing experience, and expecting them with just a day or two of training to perform as well as those who had been doing the job for years—at approximately half the pay, with no benefits and no guarantee of a job next week at that—was a fantasy.

After the temporary employee count in my department increased significantly, I stepped up my little display self-audits from several a week to dozens a shift. I found myself going back and forth from the case-packers to the display packaging area so often I was literally wearing out the soles of my shoes. And I'd hear the same excuses over and over again. "I didn't see it," "that must be from when I was on break," "the person who trained me never told me that," or the all so famous "this job is too hard. I'm just trying to make it through the night and I won't be back tomorrow anyway."

And most of them only had to ask the temp agency to assign them to another company, and they were off the hook. The temp agency's priority was not to keep us fully staffed with people we were 100 percent satisfied with. Their number one priority was to send as many temps to as many companies as possible on any given day. That's how they made their money. Their profit margin was driven strictly by quantity, not quality.

I shared these stories with anyone from management who would listen. But I was merely told to "do the best you can." This "best you can" scenario basically meant I had to resort to putting two undertrained people on one line together, hoping that what one couldn't catch, the other one would. Or putting someone on a line at the last minute, someone I had little or no confidence in, because the original temp I had scheduled for a line, who I knew was capable of doing the job properly, was constantly late or absent. And many good temp packers took plenty of time off or showed up late whenever they felt like it. They were all well aware that I hesitated to tell the agency to replace them based on attendance because people supplied by the agency who could—and would—do the job properly were hard to find. So I always had to overstaff, because I never knew from one day to the next which temps were actually going to show up.

In addition to the use of temporary employees, the cuts also meant we soon lost our benefits administrator, off-shift cafeteria and medical department services, the plant newsletter and several nonessential administration people. Despite all these drastic cost-cutting efforts, the threat of a plant closure always loomed over our heads, seeming a little more inevitable each year. And, at least in my opinion, the use of temporary employees actually added to this threat because our quality rating was now in jeopardy. The sense of job security I had enjoyed for so many years was out the window.

I started contemplating a possible career change for the first time since the tender age of 18. I had developed a long track record in machine operations, liquid and dry ingredient processing, material handling and warehousing, food processing sanitation, and mechanical maintenance, and I had spent my last six years in front line management as a team leader.

For many years I had fantasized about leaving the cold and ice of the Windy City behind for the sunshine of the South but never dreamed of acting on it, only because of the security of having a good job. Now, a move to the South suddenly seemed feasible. It wasn't until I left the friendly confines of that plant, however, that I could fully appreciate all I was leaving behind.

Section II. Myrtle Beach: A Great Place to Live But You Wouldn't Want to Work There

Chapter 4. Starting Over Isn't Easy

My wife's family had all gradually migrated to Myrtle Beach, South Carolina over the years. It had been our annual vacation spot since the time we met. My wife was actually the last holdout still in Chicago and every year we heard the same question. "Why don't you guys move to Myrtle Beach?" And my response was always the same. I have a good-paying job, job security, and benefits with a company I plan to retire from. But, with much of this appearing to be ready to fly out the window, suddenly the proposition actually started to make sense.

So I bid a fond farewell to the only city and career I ever knew and headed to Myrtle Beach, with a wife, five kids and everything we owned in tow. I set off to see if I could do what so many of my coworkers were afraid would be impossible: find a viable life after leaving that plant.

I would be part of the Myrtle Beach workforce for the next six years. Along with three different day jobs in that time, I also developed a fairly successful freelance writing career with local publications. Myrtle Beach was the land of opportunity for the un- or under-skilled and un- or under-educated. You can be anything you want to be in Myrtle Beach, so long as you're willing to do it cheap enough.

One of the big problems with the Myrtle Beach job market comes from it being such a popular retirement area. It seems some people work all their life so they can retire to the beach and play golf. Then after six months of playing golf, these same people decide they're bored. Most are hundreds if not thousands of miles away from their children and grandchildren. And believe it or not, many can't find anything better to do to occupy their time than go back to work. Unfortunately, once they begin collecting the Social Security they've worked for all their lives, they cannot make more than $1,200 a month without having their Social Security benefits penalized. So they go to local employers with nothing but time on their hands, willing to work any amount of hours, because they are willing to do pretty much anything to break their boredom and request not to be paid more than $1,200 a month. And that sets the wage base for the area, $1,200 per month, or a whopping $300 per week.

I knew there was something different about the Myrtle Beach job market from the first article I read in the local daily newspaper about how difficult it was for area employers to find and retain dependable employees. I also heard these allegations firsthand from many employers in interviews. Lazy, irresponsible, unmotivated, unreliable and worthless are just a few of the words I've heard Myrtle Beach employers use to describe their workforce. And I had more than my fair share of interviews in Myrtle Beach, even though I had one job or another with a fair amount of responsibility and challenge almost the entire time I lived in Myrtle Beach. Those jobs were mediocre at best due to low wages and inadequate benefits, so I always had at least one ear and one eye open at all times in hopes that something better would come along. The entire 22 years I had worked for that first company, I was never looking for a job. While I worked in Myrtle Beach, I was always looking for a job.

After about six weeks of job seeking, including turning down several insulting offers for $7.00 and sometimes even as low as $6.00 per hour, I began my Myrtle Beach career as a maintenance supervisor at a fairly nice oceanfront hotel. I didn't know the first thing about hotel maintenance when I showed up at the hotel's corporate personnel office to inquire about a maintenance position. But they were willing to turn the entire maintenance department over to me based on the fact that I had six years of experience as a production supervisor as well as some industrial maintenance experience. Besides that, I was willing to accept their offer of $8.75 per hour. Myrtle Beach, the land of opportunity—for the inexperienced.

Sadly, that was actually my best offer. The next closest was an offer from a small cable manufacturer who invited me to join their maintenance department for a generous $7.00 per hour. That offer helped mold my decision to apply for a position in the hotel industry. I received offers from other manufacturers as well, for everything from machine operator to lead man—for less. If 22 years of manufacturing experience couldn't command more than $7.00 per hour, I'll be damned if any of those companies was going to get the benefit of all that experience.

So I decided that, if I was going to take a shot at this Myrtle Beach lifestyle, working for peanuts, I was going to add a little flavor to those peanuts and gain some different experience to enhance my resume in the process. I went from making $19.19 per hour for supervising a department to making $8.75 per hour for doing essentially the same thing. Granted, it was a much smaller department. I had a total of five maintenance men when fully staffed versus 20-something packers, utility people and operators on my factory job. But I also had many responsibilities as a hotel maintenance supervisor that I didn't have as a production supervisor, including hiring and firing, scheduling, parts ordering, inventory control and the oh-so-glamorous and rewarding duty of dealing with guest complaints. But how many other kids from Chicago got to be greeted by a breathtaking view of the Atlantic Ocean everyday when arriving at work? At least, that was how I convinced myself to take this job.

When I arrived for my first day of work at this non-factory job, it was slightly overwhelming, although I was looking forward to working somewhere other than on a factory floor. I reported to the hotel manager; she welcomed me, reiterated how much she was anticipating all the wonderful organization and discipline she knew I could bring to what she described as a "functional but unorganized and undisciplined department," and called someone from the maintenance shop to come pick me up and give me the grand tour.

On the first day, I spent time becoming familiar with the property layout, the disorganized maintenance shop and my new coworkers. On the second day, however, I received my first lesson in how things work at a company that pays substandard wages. The big news hit when I walked through the door: one of the maintenance men had tenured his resignation, effective immediately. It seemed he was offended by the fact that the hotel manager hired a supervisor without first offering him the job.

At my old job, there was always someone upset because they felt they were more qualified than a person who was chosen for a non-bid job like lead person or supervisor. I had several such moments of disappointment and frustration myself, over the years, before my team leader ship finally came in. But no one had ever quit over it. Pouted? Occasionally. Grumbled? Sure. Bitched and moaned? You bet. But quit? Never. I guess that's the difference between a workforce that is satisfied with the overall compensation and one that is not.

This was big news only to me. No one else was shocked or even seemed to care. When I mentioned my concern over the resignation at the weekly staff meeting, I was told this happens all the time in Myrtle Beach, especially in the hotel industry where hundreds of employers are always hiring—and very few offered what would be considered above-average wages. An experienced hotel maintenance man in Myrtle Beach working for $7.00 to $8.00 per hour could quit a job today and have several offers for comparable pay tomorrow. So what was the incentive to stay? There was none. This led to disgruntled hotel employees quitting on whims all across the Grand Strand (as the area from North Myrtle

Beach all the way south to Pawley's Island is affectionately known) every day. The happy tourists who flocked there on an annual basis may have considered this corridor of vacation wonderlands "grand," but the thousands of underpaid employees trying to make a living there had much less flattering terms for this area.

Now I faced the problem of reshaping a department that was shorthanded. I was told it happens all the time in Myrtle Beach. Nobody in Myrtle Beach would ever consider something as drastic as increasing wages to fill vacant positions. They just continue to work shorthanded, doubling the workload on existing employees, cutting corners wherever possible or simply allowing things to go undone.

Number two resigned a few months later. His name was Wayne and he was our senior, not to mention most valuable, maintenance man, by far. Wayne was actually an electrician's helper from Brooklyn who, like me, came to Myrtle Beach to escape the cold of the North but was struggling with the Myrtle Beach wage scale. Wayne opted to go into hotel maintenance as opposed to continuing to work as an electrician's helper because he said in Myrtle Beach they paid the same and hotel maintenance was easier. This was a tactic that was commonly used in Myrtle Beach. Since no occupation seemed to pay more than another, many unmotivated workers chose their occupation based on the least amount of work they would be required to do. Wayne had dumbed down his electrical skills substantially because he felt no one was willing to pay fair value for those skills, similar to what I did with my manufacturing skills. But also like me, Wayne was still far more motivated than the typical Myrtle Beach employee and he did work hard.

Wayne had been campaigning for a raise for quite some time. But our GM refused to sign off on the raise, even though it was recommended by both me and the hotel manager. The GM's rationale was that he didn't give raises based on the fact that someone said he needed more money; if Wayne wanted a raise, he would have to do something to earn it. Did I mention he was our most productive maintenance man, by far? But merit in itself apparently wasn't enough for a merit pay increase in Myrtle Beach.

So Wayne took a job with one of our suppliers, driving a delivery van. Same pay, less work. And just like that, our most talented, most productive and most experienced maintenance man was gone. And just like before, no one seemed to care except for me. A lousy quarter per hour is all he wanted. And he confided in me that he would have considered staying for as little as a dime. I think all he really wanted was a little recognition. But that's too much to ask, in Myrtle Beach. No one wanted to be the one to set a ridiculous precedent like rewarding hard work and dedication with a pay increase.

With another vacant position going unfilled, I was forced to strap on a tool belt and answer service calls a minimum of three days a week to ensure the rest of the staff got their two days off a week. Overtime was strictly forbidden, regardless of how shorthanded the department was.

But the hotel manager assured me that she would not hold it against me if any of my supervisory duties that were not essential to keeping the hotel operating fell through the cracks due to my backfilling empty shifts. So even though I was hired specifically as an administrator, with specific goals and an established timeline to meet these goals, and in spite of the fact that a position of supervisor was created for me because the hotel manager felt it was imperative to bring a sense of order to the maintenance department once and for all, these goals suddenly became unimportant due to the fact that the company could not keep qualified employees and could not find suitable replacements.

At my old place of employment, which paid above-average wages, any time they had open positions to fill, more applicants would respond than the entire surrounding neighborhood could handle. Here, our personnel department ran an ad in the daily newspaper for weeks straight and netted a grand total of zero applicants. When I brought this up again at a weekly staff meeting, the general manager informed me that it was my responsibility, not the responsibility of our personnel department or the local newspaper, to find employees to staff my department. This lack of concern for excessive turnover and under-staffed departments was something I had never experienced before.

And in addition to the chaos created by excessive turnover, I also discovered a general attitude of "who the hell cares—none of us will be here much longer, either." A perfect example of this syndrome was shown one day when we received the wrong kitchen faucet from a supplier. In a large hotel with hundreds of rooms, of course it's important to keep parts as universal as possible to minimize the number of different spare parts, like washers, that must be stocked in the shop. But knowing this was the wrong faucet and someday would more than likely require new washers that we didn't have in stock, one of the maintenance men installed it in a room anyway. I asked him why he knowingly installed the wrong faucet. "What difference does it make?" he snapped back. "It's not like any of us will still be here by the time that faucet needs new washers." I would get used to hearing this over my years in Myrtle Beach.

CHAPTER 5. HELP WANTED—PLEASE

When my 90-day probationary period was up, I was a little nervous. I was working hard, but I wasn't accomplishing most of what I was hired to do because I was always busy doing the work of missing maintenance men. But the hotel manager was true to her word and didn't hold any of that against me. She gave me an excellent review accompanied by a 50¢ per hour raise. I didn't realize it at the time, but that was huge in Myrtle Beach—almost unheard of, actually. After all, Wayne was allowed to quit over half that amount.

But this was Myrtle Beach, and I was now making over $9.00 per hour. That was far too much for a simple supervisor. So a big promotion was in order to justify my now extraordinary salary. I was no longer a simple maintenance supervisor; I was now the director of engineering. Whoopty-do! I was never much impressed by titles, especially a title that was obviously thrown at me in an attempt to try to make me feel more important than I was in spite of my pathetic salary

But even more exciting than the additional twenty bucks a week was the fact that I was now eligible for company benefits. Going without medical insurance was a scary proposition, and something I hadn't had to deal with since I was 18. I couldn't wait to get to personnel and sign up. I knew the company offered medical insurance, because it was clearly stated in the ad that the company offered an excellent benefits package. The personnel director had confirmed in my initial interview that medical insurance was included in the benefits package and went as far as to describe it as "excellent medical insurance." I even read about the "outstanding medical plan" the company offered in my employee handbook.

Unfortunately, nowhere did I read—or was I ever told—that this "excellent" and "outstanding" medical insurance could be purchased for the bargain basement price of $119 per pay period, or $238 a month for the family plan! This might not sound so outrageous by today's standards, but back in 1998, I had been paying $16.75 per week or $67.00 per month for family medical insurance earlier that same year at my old job. Besides, the insurance plan offered by my old company for that $67.00 was far superior in benefits and coverage to the plan provided by the hotel which was roughly four times the cost.

I was already struggling to make ends meet; now, my nifty promotion and whopping $80.00 a month raise came to a net loss of $158 a month. After all those years of working for a company that treated its employees well, I had just assumed that when a company offered benefits to its employees, they would be offered at an affordable rate. If not, why bother? So I celebrated my 90-day anniversary by resubmitting my resume to every employment agency in town.

One day, after several months of working two men short, while I was still licking my wounds over my big benefits bust, the hotel manager called me up to her office. And for a change I received what I perceived as some good news pertaining to my fiasco of a new career. The personnel department had finally found a candidate for one of our openings. She told me he was on his way in for an interview and the final decision was mine, but warned me there was something different about this young man that I may not like. I immediately envisioned a physical handicap.

When I was summoned back to the office a little while later, there was a young man sitting at the hotel manager's desk. The manager introduced the young man to me as Steve and excused herself so we could talk. Steve stood up to shake my hand, and I looked him up and down. He was rather large framed for his tender age of 22. And he certainly didn't put on his Sunday best for this interview. Or if he did, he came from the poor side of town. He was wearing worn-out cowboy boots, old jeans with a hole in one knee, a weathered flannel shirt that was at least a half size too small for his massive frame, and his broken glasses were held together with a Band-Aid. He spoke with a heavy Southern drawl and was obviously not the most articulate member of his graduating class, but I saw no signs of physical disability as I had expected.

As we began the interview, it became clear this young man was not very well educated and perhaps was even somewhat of a slow learner. Upon reviewing his application, it was apparent he could not read or write. Almost every word on the page with three letters or more was misspelled. The questions on the application that were answered made little or no sense. Entire sections of required information were left blank. This was an obvious problem because one of my main goals discussed with the hotel manager was to improve the maintenance record keeping system at the hotel, focusing primarily on the work orders. (Maintenance men were required to fill one out after completing every job, but they often skipped it.) If I hired this man, in order to meet my goal of 100 percent completed and accurate work order reporting I would have to sit down with him at the end of every day and help him—or just take the easy way out and do it for him. I explained this as tactfully as I could and said that if I decided to hire him, I would help him with his paperwork as long as I saw honest effort on his part to eventually improve his reading and writing skills. He agreed, and didn't even appear to be offended.

We then started talking about maintenance skills, an area my uneducated applicant showed extraordinary confidence in. He went as far as to tell me there wasn't anything he couldn't fix. I asked how he could be sure of that.

"Listen here, mister," Steve said while leaning forward in his chair and pointing his confident finger in the direction of my nose, "I grew up on a farm. And on the farm, if your equipment don't work and you can't fix it, you can't work the fields. And if you don't work the fields, you don't have nothin to eat." He then stood up slowly, put both hands under his large belly that hung over his belt-less jeans, shook it up and down and proudly proclaimed. "In case you ain't noticed, it's been a long time since I ain't had no food."

I smiled, chuckled, perhaps even laughed out loud and asked him when he could start. I did so against my best judgment, of course. But after that shocking and entertaining response, I wasn't really sure what else to say. Besides, no one else wanted the job and I needed someone desperately, so I figured I didn't have much to lose.

My next dilemma was to decide on an hourly wage for Mr. Fix It. I didn't have much of a range to work with. Seven to eight dollars per hour was the going rate for hotel maintenance in Myrtle Beach. As a matter of fact, that was the going rate for almost everything in Myrtle Beach that required any skill level. And my hands were tied further at this particular hotel due to corporate policy that clearly stated that no one with less than two years seniority could make over $8.00 per hour unless they were in a supervisory position. If I started Steve out at $8.00 and he ended up being spectacular, I couldn't reward him with a pay increase for two years. So I decided I'd offer him $7.25 per hour to start, hoping he would do a good job so I could motivate him more with a 25¢ raise at the end of his 90-day probation. That would still leave 50¢ available for raises down the road. Steve jumped at the offer and seemed sincerely grateful to get it.

As time went on, Steve was a blessing and a curse all in one. Whichever one he was more of on any particular day depended on how many times I had to defend him to the general manager. Steve had issues well beyond his lack of education. He had a problem getting to work on time. He had personal issues that required him to leave before the end of his shift on several occasions. He had appearance issues, discipline issues, respect issues and most of the staff considered him an eyesore to the guests. The general manager hated him, the hotel manager pitied him, many of the housekeepers were afraid of him, and the rest of the maintenance staff made fun of him. But just as he had told me, there wasn't anything he couldn't fix.

I tried to explain to everyone that I needed Steve to take care of service calls during the other maintenance men's scheduled days off if I was going to have any chance of doing the job I was hired to do. The GM respected my authority enough not to order me to fire him, but made it clear my life would be a living hell until I did. I stuck to my guns. I was hired to bring organization, discipline and a sense of administration to an unorganized and undisciplined department, not run around with a tool belt fixing toilets and patching plaster. And if I was to have any chance of accomplishing that, I needed Steve. Steve or someone else, and no one else wanted the job—at least not for $7.25 per hour. Besides, it was nice to have one person on the entire property who wasn't constantly complaining about his wages.

It wasn't long after I had gotten everyone resigned to the fact that Steve was here to stay, whether they liked it or not, when our hotel manager quit. Again, this was just business as usual in Myrtle Beach. I discovered memos lying around the maintenance shop barely a year old that had distribution lists where the only name recognizable was that of the GM, indicating there had been at least one full cycle of turnover in the entire management staff in that short time frame.

She was replaced by a gung-ho, fire-them-all-and-start-over management type from California. He immediately let me know he had issues with my department. Ironically, most of his issues were the same as mine, revolving around a lack of general administration in the department. I explained to him that I had been at least one man short since my second day on the job, and I could not properly do my job while filling in as a maintenance man. He agreed and suggested we hire more people. Good plan. Why didn't I think of that? Of course, the first person he wanted to hire was a replacement for Steve. He had the same complaints about Steve as everyone else. He was uneducated, ill mannered, his verbal communication skills were atrocious, he was loud and obnoxious, he was a sloppy dresser, he didn't own a decent set of tools and overall he did not portray the image we wanted our guests to see. And Steve was guilty on all counts. And my defense to all charges was that he made $7.25 per hour.

In my humble opinion, Steve was exactly what they should expect at that rate. That's what I was making around 1982 or 1983 as a line stocker.

We were now approaching the year 2000 and that's what they wanted to pay maintenance men? Not that you need an over abundance of high skills and talent to be a hotel maintenance man, but you have to have at least basic carpentry, plumbing and electrical skills. We were not only competing with all the hundreds of hotels in the area but with the construction industry as well, because any good hotel maintenance man could easily qualify as a carpenter's helper, plumber's helper or electrician's helper on any of the thousands of new construction sites around Horry County.

But in spite of all that competition in a tight labor market, they wanted to not only pay near poverty level wages but to pick from the cream of the crop for it. They thought $7.00 to $8.00 per hour would buy every skill you need. And why shouldn't they? There were retired engineers, electricians, construction superintendents, accountants and high level management figures all over town looking to work for reduced wages due to the Social Security restrictions. There just weren't enough of them to fully staff every hotel in a resort area the size of Myrtle Beach. Most hotels in the area worked shorthanded all the time and just didn't worry about what didn't get done. Managers who, like me, were hell bent on getting to their administrative duties without pouring double and triple duty on their already disgruntled staffs had to resort to hiring people like Steve.

But our new leader had an answer for that issue as well, and a damn good one at that. He said we would increase our starting wages to attract the qualified people we so desperately needed. I told him that might be the way they do it in California, but he was now in Horry County, South Carolina, the land where most family men worked two full-time jobs just to stay fairly behind. But our new leader came in with even bigger dreams than mine and vowed he would make it happen. I think the GM and the corporate office are still having a laugh fest over that one.

I had been circulating my resume frantically since discovering the insult of an excuse for medical benefits, and I had adopted the "won't be my problem much longer anyway" Myrtle Beach attitude after only a short six months in this distorted labor market. And now I had a gung-ho "I'm going to change the world as you know it, with or without you" type breathing down my overworked neck. And to make matters even worse, this guy was even more disillusioned about how things could be improved at this hotel than I originally was. So defending Steve dropped down my list of priorities in a hurry. If they were so hell bent on getting rid of the only person who had applied for the job, so be it. Letting Steve go was the talk of the next staff meeting. I was congratulated by every other member of the management staff for making a wise, albeit long overdue, decision.

And I didn't even have to do the dirty work. The new hotel manager called me on my day off to tell me that Steve was late. I told him I had just warned Steve before leaving yesterday that he had the early shift alone tomorrow and it was imperative that he be on time, because there would be no one there to answer early calls otherwise. Steve wasn't the only one who seemed to have problems getting in for the early shift. It's tough to motivate people to get out of bed at six AM for a lousy seven bucks per hour. I was the only one on the maintenance crew who was never late for the early shift. But Steve was the one person everyone seemed to notice when he was late.

Anyway, I told the manager I felt Steve had had enough warnings and I would sit down with him when I came back and let him know his services were no longer required. But tomorrow wasn't soon enough when it came to Steve; the hotel manager waited for him by the time clock and did my dirty work for me, much to the delight of the rest of the staff. I just wondered how they were going to feel about it when I left and they were three men short—which I was really hoping would happen in the very near future.

Chapter 6. Take It or Leave It

There were countless employment agencies in Myrtle Beach. After my medical benefits debacle at the hotel, I made sure every single one of them had a copy of my resume. My phone rang constantly. There was no shortage of jobs in Myrtle Beach, especially for someone with a solid 22-year work history with a single company. But there was an astonishing shortage of good-paying jobs, even so.

I urged all these agencies not to bother submitting my resume for the typical Myrtle Beach $7.00 to $8.00 per hour, no benefits job, but most of them did it anyway, probably because they had nothing else available. I questioned the pay history of every company I was called for and declined to go on most of the interviews with companies known to pay in that range; it would only be a waste of everyone's time.

And I was tired of wasting my time on these "loser" interviews. They were all the same. I'd sit across the desk from some management type who would whine about how tough his job was because he just couldn't find dependable, qualified people; the few people that did work out quit shortly after a considerable amount of money was spent on training them; and the ones who didn't quit were uneducated, unskilled and unreliable. He would then go on to emphasize how much he felt someone with my experience and work history could benefit his organization and how pleased they would be if I would join them.

These whining sessions by so many hiring managers were comical. The first rule in good old-fashioned job seeker's Ed 101 is that you never discuss, in an interview, how badly you may need a job. The interviewer couldn't care less; he wants to hear what you have to offer to the company. Surely the inverse applies just as well, but time after time I would sit through interviews where the interviewer tried to play on my sympathy and apparently expected me to sell my services for far less than the fair value because he "really needed someone with my experience." He would then offer me his piddly little $7.00 or $8.00 per hour and be offended when I declined his offer, stating I would have to have more money.

That's the part I never did quite understand. I was being offered nothing short of insulting wages for 22 years of valuable experience with a spotless work record, outstanding references and a laundry list of industrial, mechanical, technical, managerial and communication skills; yet somehow the one making the insulting offer was the one who ended up offended.

Most of the employers, as well as the employment agencies in Myrtle Beach, could not understand this mentality. Apparently wage negotiation was not something often done in Horry County. Job offers were made by employers on a "take it or leave it" basis. And if no one took it, the job remained vacant until someone did, even if it meant leaving the job open for months and eventually filling it with someone not even remotely qualified (does the name Steve ring a bell?).

Another thing I couldn't seem to get through the heads of these programmed employment agency people was that I was no longer merely looking for a job. I already had a job, which meant that I had (or at least should have had, and would have had in a normal labor market) some negotiating power. I was currently making $9.25 per hour, so that was the target for interested companies to exceed. The way to lure a viable candidate away from the current employer is to offer more, not less.

Yet day after day my phone would ring and another agency would want to send me on a dead end interview for a $7.00 per hour maintenance job or an $8.00 per hour supervisor's position. One lady from an employment agency even engaged me in a heated argument over this. She insisted I go on an interview with a local manufacturing company that she described as "desperate for a strong leader for their shipping department," for $8.00 per hour. She said they had tried filling the position internally but that no one in their shipping department was capable or willing to step up and provide the strong leadership and organization they so desperately needed.

I told her I wasn't interested. I also told her I wasn't in the least bit surprised they couldn't find someone to provide "leadership" for $8.00 per hour. She became extremely confrontational. She went as far as to accuse me of being unfair and unreasonable for refusing to talk to this company based on the wages they were offering. She said they had reviewed my resume and were very interested in me. She said they really needed someone like me and would appreciate all I could bring to their organization. I told her if that was honestly the case, they would be willing to pay more than $8.00 per hour. Her hostility increased and she almost demanded I go on this interview.

So I told her I would be happy to go on the interview if she agreed to first contact the company and see if there was any way they would be willing to at least match my current salary of $9.25 per hour; otherwise, it would only be a waste of both mine and the interviewer's time. Also, I pointed out to her that the $7.00 and $8.00 per hour job offers were coming so fast from all the local agencies that I would actually have to start taking time off work if I was to go interview for all of them. So I was only accepting interviews that met or exceeded my current salary and offered full, affordable benefits.

She acted as if this was the most arrogant attitude she had ever encountered. But she reluctantly agreed. She called back the next day to inform me that the company had reneged on their offer to schedule an interview with me because they never started anyone out for more than $8.00 per hour under any circumstances.

This was no surprise. I expected it. Typical for Horry County, they wanted experience. They wanted commitment and dedication. They wanted a strong leader. They wanted someone with managerial experience and vision. They wanted someone with a proven track record. And they wanted it all for $8.00 per hour.

This reminded me of an interview I had been on a couple of weeks earlier. I was interviewing for the position of a warranty representative with a local home builder. I didn't know beans about home construction, but they got a hold of my resume somewhere and called stating they were "extremely anxious" to speak with me. The man conducting the interview told me they had dozens of resumes from people with construction backgrounds but none of them had the administrative skills that would be essential to succeed at this position. He convinced me that my minimal background in hotel maintenance would be enough to carry me through the technical aspect of this job and the benefits of my administrative skills would by far outweigh my lack of construction experience.

He went on to describe this position as an "extremely demanding one that would require a highly organized and motivated professional that knew how to get a job done."

"I just can't find anyone down here with any kind of a sense of urgency to get a job done," the desperate manager said to me. I'll never forget those words. I had heard some harsh accusations from employers about the overall workforce in this area, but this was one of the harshest. Yet there was also something about the tone in this man's voice when he said it that led me to believe he had more insight to the value of a dedicated employee than the average Horry County employer.

He really dwelled on my 22 years with my first employer. He seemed to think that the fact that a company had kept me around for 22 years was a testament to the fact that I had the urgency to get a job done that he was looking for. I attempted to explain that my 22 years on my first job was a two-way street. Not only was I a good enough employee for them to want to keep me around for 22 years, but they were also a good enough employer that I wanted to continue to work for them for 22 years. And I explained to him that this two-way relationship was what I was searching for with a company here in Myrtle Beach.

The man just nodded approvingly and seemed to understand. Finally, someone in Myrtle Beach gets it, I remember thinking to myself. So I was really beginning to believe this was the ticket I had been looking for. He then led me to the desk he was hoping would soon be mine and introduced me to the mountain of overdue paperwork that was piling up on the desk in double and triple stacks. Again he reiterated how demanding this job was going to be and how essential it was to fill it with the right person the first time.

He then told me he did not have another candidate he felt was even remotely close to me in qualifications, that basically the job was mine for the taking, and asked what minimum starting wage I would accept. I told him I would gladly accept the position for $10 per hour, a meager wage in my opinion for the work load he was describing.

But this man didn't see employment as a two-way street any more than anyone else in Myrtle Beach. Suddenly he showed his true Horry County colors. He immediately lost all his enthusiasm and mumbled something about having to discuss things with his district manager. Now he informed me they still had more interviews to conduct, weakly shook my hand, and I never heard from him again.

From that day forward, I made it a point to inquire about wages before scheduling an interview, even though it seemed to go against some sacred Horry County jobseeker bylaw.

After what seemed like a thousand more thanks but no thanks $7.00 to $8.00 per hour interview opportunities, I received a call from another agency. They wanted to send me on an interview for a quality control position with a cable and wire harness manufacturer. I had previously turned down a maintenance mechanic position with this same company because they only offered $7.00 per hour. The woman told me the quality manager was looking to completely restructure the department. He had already reviewed my resume, and if the interview went well he was willing to create a new job title within his department for me. She was pretty sure the job would pay more than that of a maintenance mechanic. Curiosity had the best of me at this point, so I agreed to go for the interview.

When I sat down with the quality manager, he immediately grabbed my attention. He described a new position he wanted to create that would be called receiving inspection coordinator. Initially, I would be responsible for supervising all the activities of the receiving inspection area, which included inbound inspection of wire, cable, connectors and various electronic components as well as the related documentation, record keeping and data entry. After I mastered this phase of my training I would also handle all supplier rejects and would continue to gradually pick up more responsibility until I eventually took over all the duties of the current quality control technician, which included equipment calibration, ESD control, management of UL and CSA standards, internal audits, evaluation of customer returns and establishing corrective action plans for customer returns and customer complaints.

What's more important, I would be part of a three-person management team, just below the quality manager, that would consist of the current quality control technician and the lead inspector as well as me. Collectively the three of us would be responsible for the restructuring of the entire Quality Control department and would ultimately be involved in every major departmental decision.

He also told me the plant was about to begin seeking ISO 9001 certification, and since I had been involved in several large scale program implementations in my manufacturing career, such as HACPP, Quality Vision, TQM and the Green Room process, he would make me part of the committee responsible for implementing an ISO 9001 program.

This was definitely the best opportunity I was presented with since arriving in Myrtle Beach. The man who I was sizing up as my next potential boss also caught my attention when he told me he realized there was a tremendous difference between food manufacturing and cable manufacturing and assured me he would demonstrate the required patience while I took the time needed to learn a whole new business. That was the deal closer for me. Sign me up, I thought.

Finally came the subject of pay. "This company doesn't pay very much," he said, broaching the same tired wage pitch I'd heard before. "I could only start you out for $7.00 to $8.00 per hour. How's that sound to you?"

I was excited, intrigued, disappointed and disgusted all at the same time. Here was a job that actually had me excited. I wanted it. I could picture myself doing it. It was more responsibility than I ever had before and probably more than I ever even dreamed of having. I would be interacting with all the upper management figures in virtually every aspect of the business, including manufacturing, engineering, sales and purchasing.

And I would eventually deal directly with customers, suppliers and agency representatives from UL and CSA. This would have easily been a

$60,000 to 70,000 annual salaried job with my original employer. But by the same token, if a position like this had existed there, they would have required someone with a Bachelor's degree in Electrical Engineering at the very least. Yet here I was, a few credit hours short of an AA in Business Administration with an outdated Certificate in Computer Operations being almost begged to take this job.

So I was torn. I wanted this job. I wanted it bad. But I wasn't willing to accept all that responsibility for a piddly $7.00 to $8.00 per hour. Somehow, I managed to muster the courage to tell the manager this. I was used to telling interviewers that by now, but not in the case of a job that I wanted so badly.

If nothing else, I thought perhaps all the experience I could gain here would eventually catapult me into a company that paid a decent wage. That is, if there were such a place in Horry County. But as I did so many times before, I stuck to my guns.

"I'm sorry," I said to the man who had been glaring at me down his nose without saying a word since his salary offer several awkward moments ago. "I can't help you. Not for $8.00 per hour. This job sounds like a wonderful opportunity and I'm definitely interested, but I have a family to support." I stood up and reached out to shake the man's hand. He looked more disappointed than I felt.

"Don't make up your mind just yet," he said after a long moment of silence. "Give me a couple of days to see what I can do."

I received a call from the agency two days later asking if I would consider a revised offer of $9.50 per hour. It still wasn't much for all they expected, but it beat what I was currently making by 25¢ per hour. And in Horry County, $9.50 per hour was one hell of an offer. Before accepting, however, I also asked about their medical insurance, including the cost. I wasn't going to make that mistake again. The manager made a call to the personnel director and confirmed that insurance was $25 per week for the family plan. That in itself equated to over a $100.00 a month in addition to the 25¢ an hour.

So with that, I accepted. And for the first time since I had met this man, I saw a full blown smile on his face. But he swore me to secrecy about my salary. He told me there were group leaders with 10 years seniority that weren't making that much, and if my starting salary ever leaked out, a lot of people would be upset.

My next order of business was to resign at the hotel. I wanted to be careful how I worded my resignation. The general manager had expressed some concern before hiring me that the pay might be an issue since I was taking a drastic pay cut from what I made at my previous job. He was concerned that I might take the job and quit shortly after because of that. So I wanted to make it clear in my resignation that the pay was not the issue at hand. (Of course I wasn't satisfied with my pay. No one in Myrtle Beach, except for maybe people like Steve, and the retirees who were working out of boredom, were satisfied with their pay.) I had agreed to take the position at the hotel for $8.75 per hour, and I was willing to do it for that amount, satisfied or not. And, I was given a 50¢ raise. Besides, it was becoming clear that I was never going to be satisfied with my income no matter where I worked, as long as I lived in Myrtle Beach.

The real issue I was resigning over was the cost of the medical insurance. In my resignation, I told them I saw their offer of insurance at that price as an insult to my intelligence. I could have purchased a family plan on my own through Blue Cross/Blue Shield at that time for around the same price I was paying through payroll deduction at the hotel. So what did I need them for?

I also told them I felt their reference to "great benefits" in their advertisements were misleading, and that, had I known the cost of their benefits up front, I would have never accepted the job. Unfortunately, after 22 years of affordable benefits with a good company, I just assumed companies had an obligation to their employees. How naïve I was!

I had other issues with their "great benefits" as well. They advertised "paid holidays." I was no stranger to paid holidays at my previous employer. They were my favorite times of the year. We got a four-day weekend at Thanksgiving every year. We received full pay for sitting at home on that Thursday and Friday; that is what "paid holiday" meant. Then, of course, the plant would also be closed that Saturday and Sunday, giving everyone four straight days off. Other holidays changed from year to year, depending on which days of the week certain holidays fell on, but we could also depend every year on having Labor Day, Memorial Day, Good Friday, the Fourth of July, Christmas and New Year's Day and there were extra floaters used to create as many three- and four-day weekends a year as possible. One time when the Fourth of July fell on a Wednesday, we actually got a five-day weekend. There were a lot of happy employees singing the praises of the company that year.

In the hotel industry, however, "paid holidays" means that if you are scheduled to work on a holiday, you get paid time and a half. If you're not scheduled to work, you get nothing. If I continued to work in the hotel industry, I would never have a long weekend again as long as I lived. I would spend the rest of my life working five days a week, week after week, year after year, and never get any kind of break unless I was sick. There were only six holidays a year on the hotel list versus thirteen at my last job. So not only would I never again see a long holiday weekend, but many of the holidays I was used to having off (with pay) would actually now be work days for straight time.

Another issue that went into my decision to bail out from the hotel after only six months was their company's inability to maintain a proper staff. I was sick and tired of letting my higher level duties fall by the wayside while I was busy doing the low-end work created by vacant maintenance positions that management was happy to leave unfilled. I was busy unclogging toilets and replacing leaking faucet washers, while trying to find time to revamp an inefficient inventory system, search for more reliable and affordable suppliers, conduct regular property inspections, reach 100 percent compliance in proper maintenance work order reporting and develop a winter preventive maintenance schedule for the off season that was just around the corner. Not to mention somehow try to fill two vacant positions that our Personnel Department had long since given up on even advertising.

Chapter 7. All Factories Are Not Created Equal

Once I put my feet back on a factory floor, I felt a little more at home. The only problem was I was still working in Horry County. The problems I had seen in small scale at the hotel, created by a high rate of turnover and non-caring attitudes, were magnified greatly here in a workforce of hundreds. The employers and employment agencies in the area, along with local newspaper reporters that wrote the annual "boo-hoo" type articles addressing the troubles Myrtle Beach employers experience with unreliable, unmotivated employees, attempted to lead people to believe that low wages were just an accepted way of life in Myrtle Beach and people in the area had learned to be satisfied. But that wasn't the case at all. As the quality manager told me during our initial interview, "this company doesn't pay very well." That sad but true statement was reflected in the attitudes of the general workforce in every department at this factory.

In spite of what the well-off minority in Horry County, the business owners, would want you to believe, low wages are seen for what they are no matter what part of the country a person was born in. When I first moved to Myrtle Beach, I was led to believe that the wages were poor because the general attitude of the local workforce was pathetic. But as I spent time working with both people born and raised in the area as well as transplants like myself, I began to realize the general attitude of the workforce was poor because the wages were pathetic.

Apparently, this generation of people in Horry County had watched their parents work their tails off in the hotels, restaurants, factories and tourist traps of Myrtle Beach for minimum wage, living paycheck to paycheck, never having any disposable income, many times working two full-time or three part-time jobs just to survive, never even earning enough money to enjoy the tourist traps they were devoting their lives to. They grew up having no motivation to develop skills, obtain an education or become loyal, productive employees because they knew it was never going to bring them a bright future. And as for the transplants like myself, who came from areas of the country that paid wages closer to the national average, it was going to take more than putting phrases like "great pay" or "exceptional wages" in help wanted ads to convince us.

But with all that being said, I looked forward to the opportunity this job presented. I was up for the challenge and ready for the responsibility. I guess it didn't hurt either to know I was one of the highest paid hourly employees in the company.

The first morning, I had a brief meeting with the quality manager and was introduced to my two counterparts, who along with me were expected to change the entire course of this minimum-wage, maximum-mess company. I was presented with the astronomical numbers in the area of last year's customer returns and was told my primary focus would be to reduce those numbers considerably—that along with revamping the receiving inspection process, streamlining the paper files, upgrading the data processing and data reporting systems, and writing ISO 9001 procedures for every single inspection, rejection, calibration and documentation process I was in charge of.

Shortly after this meeting, I was given carte blanche to wander the facility and make myself at home. My new boss also informed me that not only my wages but my title and job responsibilities as well were to be a well kept secret. If anyone was to ask, I was just an inspector in training. This way people would be more apt to cooperate with me and share information that they might not be willing to discuss if they knew I was going to be part of the management team. In other words, total deception. This was not a management technique I was familiar with, nor was I comfortable with it.

At my old employer, the first thing a new boss did was walk around and introduce himself to everyone as the new boss. There were no big secrets or guessing games. But here in Horry County, that's all they seemed to do. No wonder there was such distrust and disdain for overall management in this town. I guess there is a difference in management techniques used in dealing with a satisfied and motivated workforce versus a dissatisfied and disgruntled one.

It was more than just a little difficult to convince people I was an in-training quality inspector when I was allowed to wander the facility at will, with no assigned work area. I was the only "inspector" in the building that was called into meetings with the quality manager on a regular basis. But as lame as it seemed, my new boss insisted on sticking to the plan. He said it was imperative that no one know why I was hired until "the time was right."

But the workforce was not nearly as naïve as my new boss anticipated. They may not have known exactly who I was, but they knew who I was not. And I was not someone they wanted to draw into their inner circles and divulge well-kept work floor secrets to. I didn't blame them. I wouldn't have trusted me either, under the circumstances. Here I was, someone brought in off the street, wandering the facility at will, with no defined job duties or introductions; and people wanted to know who they were dealing with.

Most of the work done at this particular plant was hand assembly conducted by various groups at large tables. When I wasn't making a nuisance of myself on the receiving dock or in the receiving inspection office, I would wander around the tables and observe the production process, occasionally picking up a finished cable and comparing it to the blueprint. As I would walk away, I would hear the same old comments. "Who is that guy?" "What is he looking for?" Or better yet, "Are we in trouble?"

About four or five weeks after I started, the department I hadn't even officially started running yet suffered its first casualty. Our data entry clerk turned in her notice. This was a blessing for me, in a way, because I took over her duties temporarily, which took some focus off of who the mystery man was. I spent several hours a day at her old desk, punching away at a keyboard, while still making my rounds and learning what I could.

She never was replaced. Just like with the first maintenance man I lost at the hotel, many of her old duties became mine permanently. Others were pushed to different people in the department and the rest just slipped away and were forgotten. Some of these "forgotten" tasks were resurrected by the quality manager five, six months later. And of course he wanted them brought back up-to-date from the day they went MIA, which created some unique challenges.

My training was not at all what I anticipated. There was no structure; there was really no training at all. It was basically walk where you want, look at what you want, read what you want, talk to who you want and learn everything you can in the process. But I was always a go-getter and never shy about asking questions, so I was well on my way to becoming a wire and cable expert. As time went on, my official title and responsibilities were finally announced and from that day on it was full steam ahead for me.

When I dove head first into the task of reducing customer complaints, I was slapped in the face again with the turnover woes. Many cables came back simply because they were miswired—most often when someone new, with no experience, was thrown into assembly in a hurry due to production needs, and such a worker would not know how to determine where the number one position is on a connector. My first line of defense for these errors was to talk to the employees that had assembled that lot of cables and explain their mistakes to them so that it would not happen again.

Unfortunately, this solution was only good for a one-time fix. Once I sent a customer a written corrective action stating that the corrective action was to retrain employees involved in the error, whether it was in wire routing, connector orientation or blueprint interpretation, the customer expected to see no more errors of this type in the future. Unfortunately, many of our cables were produced in short runs with weeks and sometimes even months between scheduled production runs, so there were times when there would be an entirely new crew working on the next batch of cables, making the same old mistakes.

My next line of defense was at the engineering level. It was obvious that this system had to become completely idiot proof. The people in assembly were not idiots, but most were paid minimum wage and had no reason to give the job their best effort.

I spent countless hours in engineering, requesting things like more user-friendly blueprints with special notes detailing how to avoid common wiring errors and redesigned test fixtures that would prevent cables that had been wired backwards from being plugged in backwards, thus producing a false pass result. Almost every cable we produced had hit trouble after just a few months and I had to resort to more creative measures to prevent future errors.

Engineering met all these requests with great resistance. They knew that if they could pass off the responsibility to the production team, they could go on without any new effort on their own side. And it was true: it would help if we could do a better job of training and supervising the workforce. I agreed 100 percent. But since that obviously wasn't happening—and to a large degree couldn't happen—due to the rapid turnover at the facility, I had to find other avenues.

I remember one heated discussion with the senior engineering technician in the testing department who told me I was wasting my time. "This place is never going to get any better," he barked at me. "All they ever hire is housewives and students."

There was some truth to that. Myrtle Beach was all about marketing and target markets. And the factories lying on the outskirts of this tourism Mecca took lessons from the low-paying tourism industry. Where the hotels, restaurants and other tourist traps targeted retirees looking for low-paying jobs to supplement their Social Security or imported cheap labor from places like Mexico and Jamaica, this place also had a target market for cheap labor; and as the agitated man told me, it was literally housewives and students.

There was a sensible strategy to this. There was a booming construction market in Myrtle Beach during this time frame. But like the tourism and service industries that dominated the local job market and set the wage base, the construction industry refused to pay a decent wage for skill and experience. This led to a flood of self-employed construction workers in the area. Anyone who was worth a nickel went into business for himself rather than going to work for a construction company with retired carpenters and illiterate immigrants for abysmal pay. The result was a growing amount of households with well above average incomes but no access to affordable health benefits. And those are exactly the "housewives" this company embraced. The wives of self-employed men were willing to take a job for minimum wage because they could provide one thing their husbands couldn't: affordable medical insurance.

The problem was, this company had more positions to fill than the area had available housewives. So that's where the current students came in, along with numerous high school drop-outs who couldn't find other positions. The problem with the students was the same issue my previous company had when they started to use temporary employees: no dedication, no motivation and no vested interest in the long term future of this company. For the record, these minimum-wage students were also hired through a temporary agency. The process was slightly different in the sense that these jobs were advertised as "temp to hire" positions where, people had the opportunity to become permanent employees. But most of the temps who stayed for any length of time were strung along for time frames much longer than the typical 60 to 90 day probationary periods without being offered a permanent position, and they lost any motivation they may have had after a couple of months. But this company was committed to make fail-proof cables somehow, with this low-caliber workforce, and it seemed that a large part of my job was to make sure that happened.

At one point, I thought relief was on the way. The corporate office sent an employee satisfaction survey to the plant. When a similar survey was conducted by my previous employer, right after our first three-percent wage reduction, the second wage reduction was eliminated due to the response from the work force.

With all the negativity I knew would flood the pages of these surveys, I had images of massive restructuring running through my mind. I even overheard one shipping clerk tell a coworker that he made up a couple of halfway decent comments just because he didn't want to turn in a survey with nothing but negative comments. "Not me," replied the coworker. "I told them exactly how bad this place sucks. And so has everyone else I talked to."

One thing I noticed about this survey was everywhere a question mentioned anything about wage satisfaction, it was qualified with wording similar to "competitive for the region." It appeared they were buying into the philosophy that people in the South expected and accepted that their wages would be lower than in other parts of the country. But even many fast food places and gas stations in the area paid $7.00 per hour, while this place started most people out for $5.15. They weren't even competitive with McDonalds, Burger King and gas station mini-marts in many cases!

I waited patiently for the results of this survey to be analyzed and acted on. I was so anxious to see things improve. If I learned one thing from my previous employer's survey, it was that if you ask employees what is important to them and try to deliver it, they will respond with better attitudes. And better attitudes at this place would definitely mean an easier job for me and better quality output. But I obviously wasn't working for a company that worried about employee morale anymore. A month passed, then two, then six and eventually twelve, without a word ever being said. Why they even bothered to ask is beyond me. Perhaps they honestly didn't have a clue how dissatisfied their workforce was, and when they found out they just swept all the negativity under the rug.

Chapter 8. Comfortably Numb

As time went on, I found myself settling in. As far as this company was from my previous employer—it was slowly becoming home for me.

My new boss was extremely intelligent. He knew the wire and cable business inside out, and in many ways he was an incredibly valuable mentor to me. He was also a screamer. If I didn't get a project done on time, he would scream. If I rushed to get a project done on time and it didn't come out exactly as he wanted, he would scream. If I knew I wasn't going to make a deadline and asked for an extension, he would scream even louder. If I had everything absolutely perfect and on time, most times he would think something was wrong and scream anyway. In those cases I would sit there patiently, waiting for him to stop long enough to breathe. Then I would seize that brief second of silence to show him he was wrong, after which he would normally laugh and say something like, "Well now, how about that."

Of course those of us in the quality department didn't have any special license on getting screamed at. Every manager in that plant was a screamer. Our manager just happened to do it a little better than his counterparts. So virtually everyone who worked inside the walls of that facility got an earful from time to time. Those of us in quality just got it a little more often, and usually quite a bit louder.

But the humiliating tongue lashings doled out on a daily basis to hourly employees—many times right in the middle of the production floor—were often mild-mannered in comparison to the way these managers would go after one another. And just like when the enraged managers were directing their furor at an embarrassed and humiliated employee, often times when they were screaming at one another it was done right in the middle of the production floor for everyone to witness. Quite frankly, these open floor screaming sessions were the most unprofessional scenes I had ever witnessed in my long career. They would have never been tolerated at my previous employer.

Many times these tug-of-wars between department managers spilled into the general workforce as well. One such time, the entire quality department was yanked from the floor for a department meeting that had one point—and one point only. We were all told we were no longer allowed to talk to the engineering manager. That was the sole purpose of the entire meeting. Our manager qualified his remarks by saying he couldn't stop us from saying "good morning" to the man, but if any of us were caught discussing business with him, we would be written up. Of course this merely enticed the other manager to go out of his way to talk to anyone and everyone he could from the quality department for the next several weeks, making things very uncomfortable for anyone in the quality department.

But that was the second most outrageous stunt our manager ever pulled at best. He was actually infamously known for the time he lost his temper and turned over a production table—while production assemblers were working at it! I don't really know all the particulars but I heard enough second-hand accounts of the event—including from the quality manager himself—to be confident it actually did happen. One thing I do know for certain is that if anything even remotely close to this had ever happened at my previous employer, the second-hand accounts would have been about how the quality manager was fired for overturning a table while people were working around it.

In spite of all the yelling, screaming and outrageous behavior of the quality manager, however, he remained true to every commitment he had made to me. We would sit down approximately every three to four months and he would review my progress on the new responsibilities he had given to me in our last review meeting. Once he felt I had those responsibilities mastered, he would pile a few more responsibilities on me, along with a pay increase he felt was equal to the additional responsibilities I had previously mastered. In some cases the increase would be 25¢ or 30¢ per hour. Other times, it would be slightly more. The highest I remember was 65¢ in one big jump. It all depended on the amount—and intensity—of the responsibilities I was being given.

But even my low-end increases were out of the ballpark compared to what the average Joe on the assembly floor could look forward to, many of whom I had overheard complaining about the 10¢ or 15¢ per hour increase they received for an entire year.

The biggest challenge I faced with my new responsibilities revolved around the issue of customer returns and supplier rejects. More specifically, my concerns were in the area of communication. Once I was responsible for these areas, I was required to have not only written communication with customers and suppliers regarding quality issues, but occasionally telephone communication as well. And most of the people I had to communicate with at these companies were engineers who could talk circles around me when it came to electronics. This was a big concern for me. The last thing I wanted to do was make the company I worked for sound stupid.

But I quickly found a possible solution to that dilemma. One thing this company did have in common with my previous employer was an educational assistance program. And now that I was working in the electronics field and was expected to be able to discuss quality issues with electronic experts on at least a somewhat intelligent level, I decided I would show some independent initiative and go back to school for electronics technology. This aspiration was met with some tough resistance from my boss, however, much to my surprise.

Getting a supervisor or manager to sign off on an educational assistance application at my previous employer was simply a technicality. There was rarely any discussion, definitely no resistance. They would sign on the dotted line and pass it on to personnel. If employees were interested in bettering themselves, the company couldn't be happier.

My new manager, on the other hand, fought me tooth and nail all the way, doing everything in his power to convince me this would be unnecessary, a waste of my time as well as company resources. He told me specifically that there was nothing I needed to know about electronics technology that didn't apply specifically to wire and cable harnesses and there was nothing I needed to know about wire and cable harnesses I couldn't learn right there in the plant.

I didn't understand this attitude at first. But then I realized the game he was playing. He wanted me to be well-versed and knowledgeable, especially once I started having some direct contact with customers. But he only wanted me to become knowledgeable in my new field as it directly applied to what I needed to know, to do my job properly, and no more. That way I would remain valuable to that particular company, for my particular job, without increasing my marketability to other companies for other jobs.

This was another game popular in Myrtle Beach. The hell with trying to maintain a stable workforce by offering even average wages and a good work environment; just keep your training to a bare minimum so other companies won't be tempted to hire your employees away. However, I can be persistent when I see an opportunity, and I continued annoying my boss until he reluctantly approved an application to allow me to upgrade my long outdated certificate in computer operations to a current certificate in computer repair, a program that included basic electronics technology 101. My original request for company-paid educational assistance had included an Associate's Degree in Electronics Technology. But something is better than nothing, as the saying goes.

With the exception of my disappointment of not being able to take full advantage of the company's educational assistance program and having to deal with an unmotivated workforce and a screaming upper management staff on a daily basis, I was rolling right along. Within a year, I was extremely confident in my abilities when it came to overall quality control for cables and wire harnesses. Before my two-year anniversary, I was fully in charge of the receiving inspection department, customer returns—including failure analysis, and corrective actions—supplier rejects, ESD control, equipment calibration and at least a handful of other duties. I was also busy writing ISO 9001 procedures and was considered the front-running candidate to replace the quality control supervisor in two to three years when she replaced the soon-to-retire quality manager.

Unfortunately, the company's progress didn't keep pace with mine. One of our biggest contracts with a medical equipment supplier was cancelled. Our quality manager said we lost the business to cheaper foreign labor. Knowing all the issues I had to deal with from our minimum-wage workforce, I had to wonder what the quality rating would be for foreign companies that had labor costs even lower than ours. We also saw a substantial drop in orders across the board from the rest of our customers, including our largest and oldest customer.

Shortly after I celebrated my third anniversary, I was notified at approximately 3:30 on a Friday afternoon that I had a 3:45 meeting with the quality manager. I found this a little strange, considering the shift—and the week—ended at 4:00. But I assumed something urgent had just popped up, so I dropped the four or five loose ends I was trying to tie up and headed up to the front office area. Was Friday going to turn into an unexpectedly long day and perhaps even a rare Saturday spent at the office? (This company was just as strict about overtime as the hotel I previously worked for.)

When I walked into the meeting at 3:45, a few other people were already sitting in the room and the quality manager was discussing the high cost of Cobra insurance. I immediately knew this couldn't be a good thing and hesitated in the doorway. He stopped in mid-sentence and motioned me to come in.

"There's been a layoff, Clyde," he said in his usual strong and unwavering voice. "Come on in and have a seat."

So when all was said and done, at the end of that surprise "meeting," after three years of working feverously to reduce customer returns, improve receiving inspections, revamp departmental record keeping, rewrite virtually every receiving inspection and calibration procedure and play an instrumental part in gaining ISO 9001 certification for the company, I was given 15 minutes to clean out my desk and told my insurance would be cancelled at the end of the month (less than two weeks away).

The whole thing was pretty shocking to me. This was the first time I was leaving a job on someone's terms other than my own, and that included at least a half-dozen high school or summer jobs washing dishes, cooking, bagging groceries, stocking shelves and cleaning up construction sites. In the case of my first full time job, where I knew I was considered key because of my team leader position, I even gave a two-month notice to make sure they had plenty of time to decide on a suitable replacement.

The ironic part was that just months before I was blind-sided with this "meeting," I had requested a private meeting with my supervisor to discuss a personal issue. She automatically assumed it had something to do with me turning in a notice and went into shear panic. So when they thought I might be leaving on my own, in perhaps as little as two weeks, they said they didn't know how they were going to get by without me and almost begged me to stay. However, when they decided it was time for me to go, they felt they owed me no more than 15 minutes. And they wondered why there was no employee loyalty at this company.

I had been laid off on two or three occasions early at my previous employer. But the differences between the two experiences were light years apart. For starters, anytime there was the slightest hint a workforce reduction might become necessary at my previous employer, written notices were hand delivered to all employees potentially affected. These notices were required to be delivered a minimum of two weeks before the layoff was anticipated. Depending on the magnitude of the layoff, the company would notify anywhere from 25 to 100 or more people above and beyond the number of employees they anticipated actually laying off. This way, if more unexpected drops in production occurred, requiring additional layoffs, no one would be caught by surprise.

Employees affected by lay off would also usually be given an estimated date of return, rarely extending past a month or two. Layoffs were conducted strictly by seniority and employees were guaranteed to be called back in that same order of seniority. Of course, no hiring was allowed during these time periods and the use of temporary employees was strictly forbidden if even one regular employee was out on lay off.

The time people were out on layoff counted towards their seniority and all their benefits remained intact, with no increase in cost for up to a year, provided they kept up with the monthly payments, which was well under $100 per-month for full family medical, dental and vision insurance as well as life and long term disability insurance for the employee.

In the rare event a group of employees remained on lay off for one consecutive year (and if they were called back even for one week, the one-year countdown would start over again from the date they returned to lay off), the employees would be considered terminated due to a lack of available work and would then have to resort to the unaffordable Cobra option if they wanted to continue insurance coverage from that point on. But these terminations were rare. I can only remember one time in my 22 year tenure with the company when a group of employees were laid off and eventually terminated after a year had elapsed.

My previous employer also went to great lengths to avoid layoffs altogether by shifting production schedules. They also offered voluntary layoffs, where more senior employees who might want some extra time off could volunteer to go on layoff under the same conditions as the mandatory layoffs, saving a few employees at the top of the list from that fate.

But things were quite different at this company. They laid off whoever they wanted, whenever they wanted, for as long as they wanted, with no notice, no particular call back order, no guarantee of ever being called back, no freeze in hiring while employees were on lay off and no extension of benefits. It was basically, "Adios amigo, you've got 15 minutes to round up your belongings and get off our property. Don't let the door hit you on your way out!"

Back at my desk, the scene was somewhere between frenzied and pitiful. I was in frantic clean out mode, trying to decipher what was mine to take, what needed to be left behind, perhaps with some kind of explanation, and what—if anything—was important only to me and could be pitched in the trash. With a half-dozen or more projects going on simultaneously at any given time, my desk was always a mess. And my boss liked it that way. He viewed a cluttered desk as some kind of badge of honor that let everyone know how busy—not to mention important—you were. But I didn't really want to leave it that way. Why things of this nature still seemed important to me I'll never really understand.

At least my supervisor, whom I had worked closely with on many projects, procedural changes and other insanely challenging dilemmas over those three years, someone who had been at the same level as me for the first year or so when she was the quality control technician, prior to her promotion to supervisor, allowed me to leave with a small portion of my dignity intact. She said her good-byes and expressed her well wishes at my desk and refused to give me the personal escort out the door that was supposed to be mandatory for all laid-off employees, allowing me to see my own self out the same way I had every other day of my three-plus years in that building.

That was something else I didn't really understand. On the rare occasion someone was terminated at my previous employer and things got a little heated, they would be escorted out of the building as a precautionary measure. But this was never used for people who were laid off through no wrong doing on their part. Of course, when you lay people off in a cold-hearted manner, I could understand the company's concern over possible repercussions from enraged employees. But some sort of immature revenge game or sabotage was the furthest thing from my mind. I had more important concerns, like continuing to feed my family.

Chapter 9. Making Ends Meet

Myrtle Beach was full of entertainment; and I loved to be entertained. Problem was, at Myrtle Beach wages, who could afford to pay for entertainment? I found a solution to that problem. It was actually an unplanned solution, but a solution nonetheless.

One day shortly after I started working at the hotel, I walked into a sandwich shop to buy lunch. While waiting for my order, I noticed a stack of magazines marked "free" lying on the counter and picked one up. It was a local entertainment magazine. The target audience was obviously twenty-something year-olds. And based on the writing style of the magazine's content, I assumed it was also written primarily by twenty-something year-olds. I was 40. In spite of my obvious age disconnect with this publication, however, something about it intrigued me, so I tucked it under my arm and took it home with me.

I had just enjoyed my first paid writing assignment shortly before moving to Myrtle Beach. A fairly large daily newspaper in the area had editorial columnists called reader columnists. They were nothing more than the name implied. They were actual readers of the newspaper who were selected as columnists for one-year stints by way of contest. I sent in an entry in the form of a sample column the year before I moved and was selected. Prior to that little adventure, my only writing experience was as a volunteer for a plant newsletter at my previous employer.

So as I read my little freebie magazine about all the Myrtle Beach late night hot spots, along with the latest hits and most recent artists (most of whom I had never heard of), I realized I had absolutely no credentials whatsoever to write for this publication. But I loved music. And I did spend several years playing music on the bar scene in Chicago. So I decided to contact them anyway.

I found an e-mail address for the publisher, typed up a quick synopsis of my writing experience, and told him I'd like to write for his publication. Much to my surprise, after a couple of back and forth e-mail correspondences and a brief face to face meeting, he offered me the opportunity to write an entertainment column targeted at the over 40 crowd in an effort to attract more older readers. It didn't pay anything but I thought it might be fun. The publisher had a fulltime day job in marketing and ran this magazine more or less as a hobby. Approximately six months after I came aboard, the publisher decided he had pursued this hobby long enough and pulled the plug.

There was another local entertainment magazine in town I had discovered shortly after I started writing for the first one. This magazine was actually geared more towards my age bracket. So I contacted that publication and when I explained who I was the publisher recognized me and said he had been following my columns and thought his magazine would be a better fit for me than the previous one I had been writing for. He then offered me an opportunity to write a column for his magazine at a rate of $30 a column. I was thrilled, not to mention impressed. This was a small, local magazine and that $30 offer was actually $10 a column more than I was paid as a reader columnist for a major daily newspaper with a circulation at the time of right around 65,000.

As I would soon learn, almost everyone in Myrtle Beach had a second job or some kind of side gig. This became mine. It didn't bring much into the house in the form of extra money. But what it did provide was a lot of things I had always enjoyed and could pay for while working for my previous employer but now, could no longer afford. Things like free admission to concerts at the House of Blues and the Carolina Amphitheater, shows at the Carolina Opry and Alabama Theater, local music festivals and an occasional invitation to review a show at the local comedy club or the food at a new restaurant.

And the best part of this venture was I could pursue it without any interference with my day job. That's not something everyone in Myrtle Beach could say. One of our more reliable maintenance men at the hotel was also a farmer. So during planting and harvesting seasons, farming became his priority and he wasn't quite so reliable for us. But he was completely upfront about it and at least the hotel was willing to work with him.

We had several minimum wage employees at the cable manufacturer that weren't that lucky. It seemed like there were always at least a couple of second shift employees getting in trouble on any given day for being late because they also had a day job and didn't get off on time to make it to their second job on time. There were also many times when first shift employees requested an earlier dismissal time to accommodate a second shift job they had to get across town for. To the best of my knowledge, these requests were always denied.

And based on the number of second shift employees we had that were chronically late due to schedule conflicts with another job, I'd say it was safe to assume our company was far from the only one in Myrtle Beach that was unwilling to work with low-wage employees that needed to work two fulltime jobs just to survive to accommodate a second work schedule. Of course, the simplest solution to these problems would be to pay your employees a true, livable wage so they don't need to get a second job. But I wouldn't hold my breath waiting for something like that to happen in Myrtle Beach.

That's why I could never understand the whole temporary employee strategy. I certainly didn't understand it with my previous employer at a plant that had enjoyed decades of overwhelming success by maintaining a stable and productive workforce through offering good wages and benefits. And I really didn't understand it in a town full of cheap employers like Myrtle Beach because in actuality there was nothing "cheap" about cheap, temporary labor. These temporary employees may have worked for cheap wages (which explains why so many of them had bad attitudes), but they were anything but cheap to the employers.

I remember sitting in one staff meeting in particular at the hotel. The general manager told the executive housekeeper to review the role of temporary agency employees being used as fill-in housekeepers and make sure they were all essential to the operation because they were costing the company $11 per hour per employee. Not only was I there (proudly wearing my director-of-engineering nametag) along with the executive housekeeper but others sitting around the table included the food and beverage director, the front office manager and the general manager's personal secretary. From the look of shock and awe on all of our faces, I'd say it was safe to assume none of us were making close to that $11 per hour figure the GM had just thrown out. As a matter of fact, a couple of us asked for an application for a housekeeping job.

"They don't make that much," the GM replied with a chuckle. "They probably get paid minimum wage. But that's what our company pays out to the agency for them."

So I threw out the suggestion that maybe if it was so difficult to find housekeepers, and the company was able to afford to pay a temporary agency $11.00 per hour for temporary housekeepers, we should consider increasing starting wages for housekeepers to attract more reliable and motivated candidates. My suggestion was immediately dismissed as "ridiculous." So the company seemed to have no issue with paying $11.00

per hour "for" a housekeeper when they really needed one but would never consider paying $11.00 per hour "to" a housekeeper even though it would surely guarantee they would be able to pick from the cream of the crop not only on the available list, but from competing hotel staffs as well. That, in my opinion, is the true definition of "ridiculous."

And just for the record, I wasn't suggesting the housekeeper's wages be increased to anywhere near $11 per hour. I'm sure everyone seated at that table, including me, would have immediately demanded more money had the GM declared starting wages for housekeepers would be raised to $11.00 per hour. In all honesty, I was extremely offended to learn the company was paying an agency that much money for the temporary use of housekeepers that may—or may not—have been any good when I was being paid a lousy $9.25 per hour by the same company, not only to run the entire maintenance department, but to backfill empty maintenance shifts and play maintenance man as well.

So the line of thinking I threw out for consideration was if we were resorting to paying a temporary agency $11.00 per hour for housekeepers because the company couldn't find suitable housekeepers for the minimum-wage rate at that time of $5.15 per hour, perhaps an additional dollar per hour above minimum-wage might make our property a little more attractive to perspective employees, possibly even making it unnecessary to ever again resort to relying on that expensive and unreliable, temporary help. It made perfect sense to me, as well as many other staffers in the meeting—but not to the GM.

But anyway, back to my second occupation. I wrote diligently for that publication for months and then eventually years, never missing a single issue. I wrote an entertainment column called "Clyde's Side" and it actually became quite popular among local musicians and night owls that lived for the Myrtle Beach night life. The magazine was published bi-weekly so my base salary, for lack of better term, was $60.00 per-month for two columns at $30.00 a piece. I used the term base, because in addition to my bi-weekly columns I would also be offered a smorgasbord of other assignments including feature articles, interviews, concert and CD reviews and an occasional cover story, each of which would add another $30.00 to my invoice for that month. So I would almost always do at least one to two additional pieces a month. And on rare occasions I'd get the opportunity to do three or four additional pieces a month running my monthly total up to between $150.00 and $180.00 for those months.

But as much as that extra cash really came in handy on those months when I could add an extra 100 bucks or more to my pathetic Myrtle Beach salary, I still was not doing this primarily for the money. I was doing it because I liked to write. I was also doing it because I loved music and being a former local musician from the Chicago bar scene myself I enjoyed being able to help promote my fellow musical brothers and sisters. And of course, I was doing it because of the free admission and sometimes even access to restricted areas at concerts I could no longer afford. But perhaps the biggest reason I continued to do this for so long after much of the initial excitement and glamour began to fade was the fact that I was building a reputation for myself as a good, not to mention reliable, writer.

Since my move to Myrtle Beach, I was quickly becoming disillusioned with manufacturing and maintenance. And soon I found myself toying with the idea of possibly turning to writing full time sometime in the future. I knew that would never be a possibility with the publication I was writing for, even after the publisher expanded from a local Myrtle Beach publication to a regional one distributed in many of the major markets throughout the Carolinas.

Then there came an even bigger opportunity. After I had been writing for the entertainment magazine for about three or four years, the major daily newspaper in Myrtle Beach expanded into the weekly market as well with smaller publications printed once a week covering a small, targeted area as opposed to covering all of Myrtle Beach and its surrounding areas like the daily did.

This new publication was looking for writers to cover the local sports scene at the high school, middle school and local park district levels. It was such a small, localized paper, the sports page actually consisted of one sports related story per issue along with some game schedules. The initial plan was to find at least three or four different writers and rotate us weekly, similar to what they did at the daily I was a reader columnist for.

We were all assigned specific schools and/or sports to start covering and given due dates to turn our first assignments in by. For whatever reason, I was the only one that ended up turning anything in. So it wasn't long before I was recognized as the "go to guy" to get the job done and started getting assignments on a weekly basis. This was fine with me because this publication paid $50.00 an article, so a guaranteed weekly assignment amounted to an extra $200.00 a-month and occasionally $250.00 a-month on those rare five-week months.

The production manager originally told me they would have to continue to search for additional writers because everyone on the staff agreed they did not want to depend on a single "stringer," as he referred to the freelance position, every week. As time went on, however, and I continued to deliver on every deadline while others continued to drop the ball, that philosophy was eventually abandoned. Early on, the production manager would feed me a topic, along with a contact person each week. As time went on, he would send me a month's worth of topics and contacts at once and allow me to work them on my own, deciding which stories to submit during which weeks depending how I was able to work them into my schedule. It wasn't long after that arrangement was made that the production manager began to take on more responsibility on the daily side of the business and became less and less involved in the weeklies until he eventually disappeared almost completely from our publication's site and I started dealing directly with the editor. The editor must have had ultimate faith in me because at that point she basically said to me something like, "You know the teams, you know the coaches and you know the seasons. Just cover what you think the best story for the week is and I'll just expect something from you every Thursday."

Another thing this publication depended on freelancers for was photos. When I first started writing for them the production manager encouraged me to submit photos to accompany my stories. They paid $20.00 a photo. Most stories were accompanied by a single photo, but two photos per story were used on occasion and three photos per story, although extremely rare, were not completely unheard of. I saw this as a great opportunity to bring in even more extra money from my sideline career (actually, extra money was a very poor choice of words. Even when I was working fulltime at the cable manufacturer, my most lucrative position in Myrtle Beach, and writing for two separate publications, I still wasn't making anywhere near what I was making at my previous employer. So there really wasn't anything extra about any money I was making).

Taking pictures for publications wasn't new to me. I had been submitting photos to go with my stories in the entertainment magazine for years. I didn't get paid anything extra for them, other than reimbursement for the cost of my film and processing. But I did it primarily as an extra service for a magazine I really enjoyed writing for and felt like I was a big part of. Not to mention, I really got a kick out of seeing my photos in publication.

My pictures looked awesome in that magazine. Two of them were even selected as cover shots. I was turning into quite the fancy photographer, if I do say so myself. Or so I thought. At the magazine, where I was basically giving my photos away, I was competing with no one. At the newspaper, on the other hand, where they paid for photos, true professional photographers were submitting photos as well and my amateur photos never found their way into the newspaper's pages to accompany my words. I suppose a more level-headed person would have realized he was in over his head and bowed out after a couple of rejected submissions. But not me, I continued to submit photos every week because I really wanted that additional 20, 40 and possibly even 60 dollars. And more so than wanting it, living in Myrtle Beach and working for Myrtle Beach wages, I really needed it.

Then the paper made a change in pay policy for photos. Instead of $20 a photo, they revised their freelance photo policy to a flat rate of $25 for one or more photos per issue. Around that same time my photos were suddenly published in almost every issue. So either my photography skills improved vastly almost overnight or the "real" photographers found it no longer worth their while to submit photos for purchase.

It wasn't like the paper suddenly dropped all their standards for photos with their price reduction. I remember one article I wrote in particular on a high school basketball team. I wanted to make action photos the theme for that particular article and shot an entire roll of players running, jumping and shooting. The digital age had arrived at this point, but not for me. I was still using film at this time (as were a lot of real professional photographers). So I couldn't view the photos before leaving the game. But with 24 images burned onto the film, I just knew I had at least five or six high quality, publishable photos.

So I went into a bit of a panic when I picked up the pictures at the photo lab the next day and realized I didn't have even one good, clear photo. After the initial panic wore off, I reevaluated the situation and decided that I actually had at least three or four pictures that, although were far from perfect, might be good enough to get by. So I submitted them as usual and kept my fingers crossed. And the editor planned on using them because she didn't have any alternatives. Then I received an e-mail from her saying the photo editor pulled rank over her and refused to let her run the photos because they were too blurry. She also included a note of encouragement at the end of the message telling me good, crisp action shots were tough to get and told me to stick with it, assuring me it would come with time and practice.

I also came up with my own plan B to make sure that didn't happen again. Although action shots were always my photos of choice, I always made sure I snapped at least a couple of still shots of an idle shooter at a free throw line, a batter in his stance at the plate or something as simple as a couple of players sitting on the bench, just to make sure I had something that wasn't blurry. From that day forward, I always had at least a few acceptable photos to submit, even if some of them were rather... well—boring.

I must admit, the whole thing was actually a little overwhelming at times. Every single week I had to decide on a story, set up an interview with a coach or a player, find time to drive to a game and take pictures, get the film developed, decide what photos to submit and come up with captions for them. And, of course, find time to write the story. And all this was on top of putting in my 40 hours on my day job, keeping up with my bi-weekly entertainment column and trying to find time to spend with my family. But that was just a way of life for many in Myrtle Beach. And those that had to try and juggle two fulltime jobs had it far tougher than I did.

I could have lightened the load considerably by dropping my commitment to supply photos to go with my stories. Many of my interviews could be conducted over the phone without me having to leave the house. Photos, on the other hand, could only be obtained one way, I had to go somewhere and take them. I lived in the heart of the Myrtle Beach area about five miles from the ocean. The newspaper covered primarily the western section of the county. So the majority of these games were 30 to 45 minutes away. But as much as dropping that part of my freelancing would have made my life easier, I knew the paper was now depending on me as pretty much the sole contributor of sports photos and I wasn't one to just drop commitments when I knew people were depending on me. Not to mention, I didn't want to let loose of that $25.00 a-week. It might not have been much on its own but when I looked at it in the perspective of $100.00 per-month it took on a whole new identity. That paid roughly half of my electric bill every month.

Looking back, I would imagine the professional photographers in the area that appeared to be boycotting the paper due to their price cuts probably looked at my photos and scoffed. I would get some really good shots often, not to mention a real gem from time to time, but I knew compared to the real professionals around town my photos were subpar. I would also imagine the pros viewed me in the same light as I viewed the retired population working in Myrtle Beach as someone trying to pick up additional income for whatever rate is offered, whether appropriate or not, and in the process, dragged down the wage base for the entire area.

But I couldn't be concerned with that. Maybe I should have, but I couldn't. I had five hungry children at home. And my chosen profession of manufacturing was no longer providing everything they needed. So I had to make up the difference wherever I could.

Then came my untimely exit from the cable manufacturer. I almost immediately started contemplating the possibility of turning to writing fulltime for the newspaper. I had been doing some research and reporters for small weeklies didn't make a lot of money. The starting range at that time was somewhere around 20 to 23,000 dollars per-year. And that usually included add-ins like personal vehicle usage allowances. The base salaries at most of the small weekly publications I researched were around $19,000.

At the high-end of $23,000, I would have been pulling in close to what I was making at the cable manufacturer. But, of course, I would also be giving up my additional income from the paper. But then I thought if I could actually get an offer near that $23,000 high-end, I might actually be able to get them to sweeten the pot a little based on the fact that I was already a reliable contributor to the paper with a proven track record for over a year at that time.

So I approached the editorial staff and informed them I was now available fulltime if they were interested. I must admit I was a little shocked when they immediately dismissed the option without appearing to put any thought or consideration into the proposition at all, stating there was no room in the budget for another fulltime staffer. I may have been surprised at the time, but looking back I suppose I really shouldn't have been. Why would I think they would be willing to offer me a fulltime salary, supply me with a desk, computer and phone line and possibly even pay me a mileage surcharge for driving my own vehicle to interview coaches and photograph games when I was already providing them everything they needed for their sports page for $75.00 per-week?

Chapter 10. A Different Way of Making a Living

The last place I wanted to find myself was on the Myrtle Beach employment available list. It was difficult enough to find a decent job offer when I was employed and felt like I had some negotiating power. Once I was officially "unemployed," however, the offers really got pathetic.

Manufacturers were few and far between around Myrtle Beach to begin with. And I don't think there was more than a small handful left that I hadn't already received a $7.00 or $8.00 per hour job offer from. So there I was, suddenly thrust unexpectedly into a full time job search with nothing but time on my hands to go on interviews and absolutely no one left in town I wanted to interview with.

After what I originally thought of as a well formulated Plan B at the newspaper went down in flames, I started sending out dozens of resumes a week. Just for kicks I sought out as many ads to respond to as I could find that asked for salary history and/or salary requirements. Remarkably, I didn't receive responses back from the vast majority of them when I disclosed my last position in Myrtle Beach paid close to $12.00 per hour and I was seeking similar wages for my next position.

Unemployment compensation rules clearly stated a person remained eligible for compensation as long as they did not turn down a job equal to their last position. And seeing how virtually no one in Myrtle Beach, or its surrounding areas, paid anywhere close to my previous position, I could have easily qualified for extension after extension of unemployment compensation benefits.

But I didn't work as hard as I had worked, to build the resume I built, just to become a professional unemployment compensation recipient. So after a few unsuccessful months of searching for a suitable manufacturing position, I again turned my attention to the low-paying but oh so prevalent Myrtle Beach tourism industry. After several disappointing at best, and insulting at worst, job opportunities, I again sold myself out to the highest bidder in this pathetic labor market. This time it was on a casino boat. I never would have seen that one coming.

If nothing else, I was at least adding another new category to my quickly expanding resume. In addition to machine operator, line mechanic, team leader, quality control coordinator and supervisor, I could now add the title of technician, slot machine technician, to be exact. Just like my director of engineering title at the hotel, it may have sounded impressive, but I could only be so impressed for a measly $9.50 per hour. I tried my hardest to drive the offer up to $10.00 but the hiring manager told me there was no room for negotiation. It was one of those infamous "take it or leave it" Myrtle Beach offers.

So after all the hard work I did with the cable manufacturer to drive my wages up to an almost livable range, I was right back to where I started three years ago salary wise. And as far as benefits went, they were worse than the "great benefits" offered at the hotel, if for no other reason, because the family medical benefits package offered by the casino was even more unaffordable than at the hotel. This time, however, at least I knew this ahead of time—but only because I inquired. It wasn't like the company disclosed that their family insurance plan was unaffordable as part of their formal interview process. I've always been familiar with the old saying "take one step forward and two back" but this was becoming more like take 10 steps backwards, then take 10 more.

The real irony of this again, just like with the hotel business, was the casino business, which I knew absolutely nothing about, made me a better offer than any of the manufacturers in the area in spite of 22 years of food manufacturing experience and another three years in cable manufacturing. Or in other words, a grand total of 25 years of experience encompassing everything from basic utility work, machine operations, dry ingredient and liquid processing, sanitation, shipping and receiving, mechanical maintenance, front line supervision, quality control, final inspection, failure analysis and corrective action and I couldn't find a manufacturer anywhere within approximately a 100 mile radius of Myrtle Beach willing to pay more than $8.00 per hour for the whole package.

To the defense of the manufacturers, I suppose, most of those $8.00 per hour jobs did come with an affordable family benefits package. Unfortunately, the problem was I couldn't afford to work for $8.00 per hour while supporting five children. Affordable benefits were only valuable to me in a job offer if the company also offered a livable wage. Otherwise, the affordable benefits package was worthless. After all, what good is medical insurance for your kids if you can't afford to keep them fed and clothed? The possibility of them needing expensive medical attention was basically a 50/50 crap-shoot. The fact that they would need food, clothing and shelter on a daily basis, on the other hand, was an absolute certainty. So I had to go wherever they were willing to pay me the most money.

Having no experience what-so-ever in a casino, other than occasionally gambling in one, I wasn't sure what to expect out of this job. I anticipated working somewhere in a small electronics shop, possibly on land and apart from the boat, where malfunctioning equipment was brought for testing and repair. But that proved to be a misdirected assumption.

Most real casinos have a position called attendant in the slot machine areas. These attendants are basically customer service reps. They perform simple customer duties such as providing change, paying jackpots above the amount automatically paid out by slot machines and filling empty coin hoppers. On casino boats, however—or at least the casino boats in Myrtle Beach—these customer service duties are performed by the so-called "technicians." We were responsible for repairing malfunctioning machines as well, but these duties were considered secondary to customer service, making it next to impossible to do any actual technician work due to continually having to stop in the middle of troubleshooting any time someone hit a jackpot, had a dollar bill stuck in a bill changer or a coin hopper ran out of coins. This didn't seem to bother most of my co-workers for whatever reason. Perhaps it had something to do with the fact that most were promoted through the ranks after working as deck hands or security guards and knew very little about being real technicians. But it drove me crazy. Just like at the hotel when I felt like I was somehow cheating the system by doing primarily maintenance man work when I knew I was hired for a supervisory role, I felt like I wasn't fulfilling my duties on the boat paying out jack pots and filling empty coin hoppers when I knew there were malfunctioning games on the boat not getting the attention they needed when it was supposed to be my job to fix them. All in all, the work really wasn't that difficult for the most part. But it certainly wasn't what I anticipated either.

Working on a boat that traveled three miles out into the Atlantic Ocean to conduct business also brought about some unusual circumstances as well. First of all, there was no such thing as leaving early. Once you were there, you were there for the duration. Not that this was a real issue for me. I never was one for asking to leave early. But it was just a little unnerving at times to know that was never an option, even in the case of an extreme personal emergency. And of course there was no such thing as being late either. If you were unfortunate enough to get that rare flat tire or hit that occasional bad accident that shut the entire roadway down for 30 minutes on your way to work, you could kiss your whole day's pay good bye. The boat sailed on schedule—with or without a full crew.

There were also those unpleasant times where rough seas rocked the boat to the point that seasick passengers would be vomiting all over the casino. And of course wherever you have alcohol and gambling you have intoxicated and sometimes unruly patrons to deal with, especially on Friday and Saturday nights.

Then there was also an issue with shifts. Due to the duration of cruises, shifts were only six hours. So this meant in order to have the standard two days off a week and still maintain full-time hours, the average person had to work one to two double shifts a week. Not that 12 hours was an incredibly long time to work, but the problem was the approximately two and a half hours in between cruises that was considered off time. So in order to log 12 hours, I had to be away from home about 14 and a half, in addition to my travel time. People who lived near the boat dock went home in between cruises and spent time with their families. But for people like me that had approximately 45 to 50 minutes travel time one way (double that sometimes during peak tourist season), going home between cruises really wasn't an option.

But even more aggravating than the standard six hour shifts was what I dubbed short shifts. On the first day of every month, all slot techs were required to show up at six AM (even if the first day of the month was a Sunday and you worked the Saturday night shift, which docks at approximately one AM, or if it was supposed to be your day off) for what was called the drop. The details of what "doing the drop" consists of aren't really important. What is important, however, is this drop was usually completed in two to three hours, occasionally even quicker. So for someone like me that had almost two hours of driving time involved in getting to work, it just wasn't worth my while to show up for that little bit of time for $9.50 per hour. But that didn't matter. It was mandatory. And if you were off for the day cruise but scheduled to work the evening shift, it meant driving all the way in for two to three hours, driving all the way home, and driving all the way back again four or five hours later.

Again using my original employer as a benchmark, their policy was clear on these issues. If an employee was required to show up at the workplace for any reason, they had to be paid a minimum of four hours regardless of how long they were actually there. If they asked to go home on their own, then, of course, they were paid only for the time they were there. But if they were required to be there and were sent home by management before four hours were up for any reason other than personal choice, illness or disciplinary reasons, the company was obligated to pay them for four hours.

I assume this procedure was put in place to stop supervisors from doing stupid things that would be detrimental to employee morale like bringing their entire department in on a Saturday for an hour meeting. But this happened on this boat all the time. I remember one time in particular. I paid a babysitter $10 and burned approximately $5 in gas (back when it was under $2.00 a gallon) to drive almost two hours on my day off to attend a mandatory safety meeting that lasted exactly 30 minutes. So if you do the math, I spent $15.00 to earn $4.75, not to mention wasting over two hours of my time on my so-called day off. Something is definitely wrong with this picture. I brought this to my manager's attention. He apologized but that's as far as it went. I explained my original employer's minimum four hour policy to him and his response was something like "Well, you won't ever see anything like that here."

There was also a little thing called the jump policy. A standard tour schedule was two slot techs during the week and three for weekend tours. Passenger counts were taken just before the boat sailed and if there were less than 100 passengers for a weekday cruise, or less than 200 on a weekend cruise, the tech with the highest hours worked so far that week was required to jump ship. Or in other words, go home after logging one hour and earning a whopping $9.50. And to make matters even worse, if this was a day cruise and you were scheduled for a double shift that day, you had to go home and drive all the way back for the evening cruise.

I could write entire chapters on all the things that I found objectionable with this low-paying, no benefits job. But there were three incidents in particular that really boiled my blood. The first came at Christmas time. Just like at the hotel, the casino didn't shut down for holidays and somebody had to be there. We worked a rotating schedule and it just so happened I was scheduled to work Tuesday and Wednesday night that week, which also just happened to be Christmas Eve and Christmas Day. Oh well, that's the luck of the draw sometimes.

I showed up at the boat on Christmas Eve as merry as I could possibly be considering I knew the rest of my family was at my Mother-in-law's house celebrating away. And apparently I was far from the only person in Myrtle Beach with somewhere better to be on Christmas Eve because we only had around 60 passengers so I had to jump. By the time I got off the boat and drove all the way back to my end of town, I arrived at my Mother-in-law's house just before everyone was ready to call it a night and start heading home. But hey, at least I made $9.50 for all my efforts!

Then came Christmas Day. Christmas celebrations in our house normally consisted of a long, lazy day of fun and relaxation, followed by an early evening dinner. This year, however, due to my evening work obligations, we had to rush through the day and my wife ran around like a chicken with its head cut off to complete a full, holiday meal for a family of seven, several hours earlier than she ever had it ready before.

After leaving a jubilant Christmas celebration with my family that was still in full swing, I arrived at the boat to find a hand-written note on the office door that read "this evening's cruise has been cancelled due to rough seas." Talk about seeing red! And this wasn't any kind of Merry Christmas type red. And unlike Christmas Eve, I didn't have to sit on the boat for an hour then jump off so I bailed out on my family Christmas celebration, drove two hours counting my return trip home, wasted a lot of gas, and didn't even get the lousy $9.50 I would have gotten on a jump cruise! I immediately called my boss on his cell phone and let him know I was not a happy camper. Had this been just another Wednesday night, I would have taken it in stride. But seeing how this was Christmas Day and most people would have preferred not to work anyway, the least they could have done was called everyone scheduled that evening and let us know we didn't have to come in instead of allowing everyone to drop whatever they were doing and drive all the way to the dock just to find a hand written note that basically said "you came for nothing, go home." Again, I received an apology but no offer of compensation for my time. I've always considered my time one of the most valuable entities in my life and my patience was quickly wearing thin when it came to it being wasted so haphazardly with absolutely no regard by this company.

The following week was New Years. This time the rotating schedule actually worked to my benefit as New Year's Eve and New Year's Day were my scheduled days off that week. Or so I thought. My boss informed me that New Year's Eve was a mandatory working holiday for all employees in the casino business and no one—in this casino or any other one in the world—could have New Year's Eve off. I found it interesting that he used the term "working holiday" to justify not giving me my scheduled day off but when I inquired to see if we would be getting paid time-and-a-half for holiday pay, he told me no — because it wasn't an official holiday. And as for my second scheduled day off that week, New Year's Day also just happened to be the first day of the month and there was this little thing called the drop that had to be attended to. You would think that, given everyone on the entire boat not only had to work the night before but the boat docked two hours later than normal, coupled with the fact that New Year's Day was a holiday and everyone had already forsaken their New Year's Eve for the company, they could push the drop back one day for just that one month. You could think that. But of course, you would be wrong.

Boiling point number two, to this day, stands out in my mind as probably the strangest on-the-job encounter I ever experienced. It was suppose to be my day off and I was preparing to take my youngest daughter fishing. As we were about to walk out the door, I received a phone call from my boss. He informed me there had been a fire on the boat the night before and it would be out of commission for some time. He said another boat was being sent as a temporary replacement but it had several outdated games and slot machines. So we needed to take some of our more popular games off our current boat and store them until the replacement boat arrived, at which time we would install them on the new boat. I told him I was just on my way out the door to take my daughter fishing for her very first time, something she had been asking me to do for a couple of weeks, and I really didn't want to renege on that at the last minute but I could come in early in the afternoon. He told me not to worry about hurrying back because we wouldn't be moving the machines until after dark. South Carolina can be a hot place in the middle of the day so it wasn't unusual for tasks involving strenuous activity to be scheduled for early morning or early evening to avoid the heat of the day. But waiting until after dark seemed just a little strange.

I received another call telling me the boat was being towed to a different dock and we were to meet the boat there at 10:00pm to remove the games. Shortly after the boat arrived, the scene turned to chaos in a hurry. The business manger was on the sidewalk (apparently acting as some kind of look-out) and as people started coming off the boat with dollies loaded up with slot machines he started screaming for everyone to hurry up and get the machines loaded into the back of a U-Haul as quickly as possible. Land-based gambling parlors were all over Myrtle Beach at one time but had recently been outlawed in South Carolina. I assumed the casino boats in the area had some type of permits allowing them to have the recently outlawed gaming machines in South Carolina. But I assumed wrong. As I found out that night, the machines were allowed on the boats because they technically were not on South Carolina land while perched on a floating boat. But they were highly illegal to have on South Carolina soil, even if owned by a casino boat. So technically, the company was instructing us all to engage in illegal activity and possibly even endangering us to the risk of arrest.

As soon as I realized all of this, I wanted to immediately leave. Wanted to, thought about it, knew it would be the right thing to do—but didn't. And that bothers me to this day. First, I think I was in at least a slight case of shock. The company I worked for was actually telling me to break the law. Even worse than that, actually, they were instructing me to break the law, without ever actually telling me I was breaking the law. Now exactly how "illegal" this whole deal was I'm not sure. And the chances of all of us actually ending up in jail over simply doing what our employer told us to do was probably pretty low. I mean it wasn't like we were selling drugs on the street corner or pimping for prostitutes. We were merely moving equipment from our workplace to temporary stor-age. But apparently because the equipment we were moving happened to be gambling equipment, it was technically illegal, even though we worked for a legitimate casino. So I don't know exactly what the odds were that I could have actually ended up in jail by doing what my em-ployer instructed me to do. My guess is they were pretty low. But I do know what the chances of possibly ending up in jail for following your employer's instructions should be. They should be ZERO!

The whole thing came down to desperation. I didn't ask to leave. I didn't object to what I was told to do. But I knew if I had, there was a good chance I could be jeopardizing my job. And that was a chance at this point in my life, after working so long for depressed Myrtle Beach wages and living paycheck to paycheck, I couldn't afford to take. For the first time since arriving in Myrtle Beach approximately five years ago, I knew exactly what the locals in this area were going through all their lives.

Strike three occurred right on the cusp on my first anniversary. I was talking with another tech just before the ship sailed. Our boss walked up with a stack of papers in his hand. He handed each one of us a copy. "Don't blame me," he said as he started walking away. "I'm just the messenger."

I glanced down and noticed the paper said something about appro-priate dress code. My eyes were immediately drawn to a line around the middle of the document that stated "Mustaches must be neat and trimmed. Beards are not permissible." I thought it nice of them to fill me in on this information a year after I had been working for them, sporting a full beard the entire time.

I immediately inquired with my boss as to any possible grievance pro-cedure the company had in place but I figured that was a shot in the dark at best considering the company didn't even have a written rule book or any kind of employee hand book. And I was right, no grievance policy at this company. Or any of the companies I worked for since leaving my original employer, for that fact. But I told my boss I felt like this "new and improved" dress code should not apply to me since I was hired with a beard. He told me to type something up and he promised me he would get it to the right people.

So I wrote a one-page challenge to the policy, to the point but polite and professional, pleading my personal case as well as trying to debunk this myth that men with beards somehow appear to be less professional. It read as follows.

> I would like to request an opportunity to respectfully voice my opinion on the new Personal Appearance of Em-ployees policy that has recently been distributed to em-

ployees. Specially, letter (f), "Sideburns and moustaches should be neatly trimmed. Beards are not permissible."

I understand, as well as agree with, your concern that employees must present a "professional, business-like image" to their customers. I do not, however, understand why this company feels a professional appearance can be maintained with neatly trimmed sideburns and moustaches yet suggests the same professional appearance cannot be maintained with a neatly trimmed beard such as the one that I have proudly worn for the better part of the last 20-something odd years.

My professional appearance was not questioned a year ago when I arrived at your office for my initial interview with a full, neatly trimmed beard. Nor was it questioned or commented on when I was photographed for all my company documentation, including the photo ID I wear daily. And to the best of my knowledge, there have been no complaints or negative comments made about my personal appearance over the last year by customers, co-workers or the management staff here, in spite of the fact that I have worn a full, neatly trimmed beard this entire time.

When a customer is paid a jackpot or finds themselves at a machine in need of service, whether the person who comes to perform the service has just a simple moustache, a full beard or no facial hair whatsoever matters to the customer about as much as rather the waitress who brings them their drink has short hair or long. As long as the person's appearance is neat and clean overall, and more importantly the service is provided in a professional and expedient manner, the customer will feel they have been treated professionally. Many men of the highest professional stature, including doctors, lawyers, politicians, famed authors and the president of this corporation, just to name a few, wear neatly trimmed beards without detracting from their professional appearance. The key to the whole concept is the two simple words, "neat" and "trim." If this policy is being instituted to target a few individuals who do not keep their beards "neat and trimmed" might I suggest that management approach those "few individuals" to rectify the unacceptable situation on an individual basis in the same manner that would be used if an individual reported to work unbathed or wearing inappropriate clothing.

Many of us here in this location are still struggling to overcome the financial hardships brought about by the unfortunate fire. In addition to this we are also in the height of a forced jump season, where many people take the time and effort to get ready and commute to work just to be sent home against their will on almost a daily basis with no extra compensation offered by the company for their time. So employee morale at this location is already in a low cycle. Instituting a policy against beards, no matter how neat and trim they are kept or no matter how long a neat beard has been part of an individual's personal appearance, will only serve to bring employee morale even lower for the individuals directly affected, while providing absolutely no measurable improvement in either customer service or employee performance to the company. I hope, based on the respectful objections I have voiced you will take the time to reconsider this policy before instituting.

Thank you for allowing me the time to express my concerns.

My challenge was praised by my boss for its professionalism and well-stated points. He also told me the challenge was well-received at the corporate office and they felt it was worthy of a written response, which I would be receiving shortly.

But again, beyond all this, the bottom line was that a company which was under-paying me and failing to provide adequate benefits felt they should be able to control me to the point of dictating my personal grooming habits. Now, don't get me wrong, I absolutely believe a company has the right to demand good grooming from employees as it applies to proper hygiene, appropriate clothing and neat appearance, and I had absolutely no issue with them expecting me to keep my beard neatly trimmed and properly groomed (something I always did anyway). But to throw a blanket statement out like no beards allowed, rather neat and trimmed or not, in an industry that already has an inability to attract qualified people due to inadequate pay and benefits seemed to me like shrinking an available pool that is already pretty small. (I was the only so-called "technician" on that boat other than our manager that had any previous electronics experience. As I stated earlier, most were promoted from within and were previously deckhands or security guards with no electronics background).

I had been through this same scenario with the hotel. But at least to their credit, they explained their no beard policy in my initial interview at the corporate office before even sending me to meet with the hotel manager. In this case, there were at least a handful of men that had been working on this boat with partial, as well as full beards, and just like that, everyone was supposed to run home and shave.

Had this been a worthwhile job, I wouldn't have as much as hesitated. I was always willing to do whatever it took to support my family as long as it was absolutely morale, reasonably safe and completely legal (except, of course, for a little late night slot machine shell game).

But in this case, I was underpaid, had no real benefits to speak of and didn't really care that much for the work. Not to mention I was becoming increasingly frustrated by the fact that my writing for the entertainment magazine was being interfered with due to all the night and weekend shifts this job required and I was missing out on many opportunities to attend concerts and other entertainment functions as a representative of the magazine. Yet I was being asked (if you consider something described as mandatory as being asked, that is) to give up something that had been a large part of my appearance since I was roughly 19 that had absolutely nothing to do with my job performance. And I was being asked to do this for a company I didn't particularly like. And a company that showed very little—if any—appreciation for their employees.

And this supposedly was all being done for the sake of professionalism. That was the funny thing about these low-paying Myrtle Beach companies and their view of "professionalism." They understand the word completely when it comes to what they expect from you. Dependability, loyalty, dedication, experience, good appearance, strong customer service—you name it, they want it. But when it comes to what they feel they owe you, there is nothing "professional" about that. It's all about pay as little as possible, offer as little as possible, provide as little as possible and demand the moon, the stars and the sun. To illustrate this point further, the hotel and casino had far more in common than just a no beard policy. They were not only the only two companies I had ever worked for that enforced such a policy but they also just coincidentally happened to also be the two lowest paying jobs and the only companies I ever worked for that offered a family medical benefits package that the average hourly employee literally could not afford. And the demands made by these two, as well as virtually all other tourist industry based companies in town were astronomical. Not only did they demand total control over an employee's appearance but they expected employees to work nights, weekends, holidays, spilt shifts, double shifts—many times for no extra compensation. They were quick to humiliate, slow to praise and rarely doled out pay increases. And as much as they complained about high turnover and poor attitudes, they offered virtually nothing to promote employee longevity or morale.

I never saw the written response to my challenge from the corporate office my boss promised me. But he never saw me without a beard either. This was the straw that broke the camel's back for me. I decided I was going to keep showing up with a beard until they sent me home because of it. I was never much of a rebel, especially when it came to the job that was feeding my family. But in many ways, I may have been turning into the typical challenge the course at every corner Myrtle Beach employee I was constantly hearing employers in the area whine about. But I worked for almost a full year for this company while wearing a beard and my appearance was never once questioned. Then all of a sudden—completely out of the blue—someone, somewhere, decided I looked "unprofessional" and I wanted to know why. I was sick to death of being underpaid, unappreciated and bullied in this "everything for the employers, nothing for the employees" labor market. I should have taken that stand the night of the illegal slot machine merry-go-round.

Section III. Welcome to Third-World America

Chapter 11. Drastic Times, Drastic Measures

As much as I enjoyed living in Myrtle Beach, it was the land of the $7.00 per hour jobs, and it became apparent I was not going to be able to successfully support a family there. That obvious fact, coupled with the ticking time bomb fuse I had lit at the casino boat with my refusal to cooperate with the no beards policy, made me realize it was time to broaden my horizons. So I started expanding my job searches to include more industrious areas of the Carolinas. I ran across an ad posted on a Charleston website for maintenance people with food manufacturing experience willing to relocate to a brand new, World Class cook facility in Georgia.

Georgia was definitely not in my original job search target range. But curiosity got the best of me and off went my resume. I received a phone call within hours and before we hung up I had received an all expenses paid invitation to come down and tour the facility. There wasn't much to tour in the facility itself. The cook plant was still a construction zone. The maintenance manager did take me through what was soon to be the cook plant facility, trying the best he could to explain what the facility would look like in full operation. He also took me on a brief walk through of the existing facility but continually reminded me that the cook plant was going to be a brand new state of the art facility that would have nothing in common with the outdated old facility.

One observation I couldn't help but notice, however—and the maintenance manager pointed out without me mentioning—was the fact that with the exception of a few maintenance guys and upper management figures, the workforce in this facility was exclusively Hispanic. He told me the company favored hiring Hispanics because they worked cheaply and did not demand any benefits. Again, I didn't ask, but apparently he felt some type of explanation was necessary. Initially, I wasn't sure if I wanted to be associated with a company that took advantage of people like that. But I was also looking to escape the Myrtle Beach job market where taking advantage of workers--Hispanic, American, retired or otherwise—with low wages and no benefits was a way of life. So I made a quick decision right then and there that if they offered me a fair deal, I wasn't going to worry about how the rest of the workforce was treated. That's not a decision I'm proud of, for the record. But sometimes drastic times call for drastic measures. And desperation will sometimes force us to abandon rational thinking. And desperate was exactly what I was after five years of abuse in the Myrtle Beach job market. The sad part was, for as many people as I heard complain about working in Myrtle Beach, they all had pretty much given up hope on any resolution. They had all resigned themselves to the fact that things were as good as they ever were going to get and there was nothing they could do about it. I could understand this hopelessness if we were talking about the former Soviet Union or China—but Myrtle Beach? It may be a great place to live—but it's not that great! This was still America, after all, and despite all my failed efforts to find an employer that offered acceptable wages and adequate benefits, no one but myself could force me to stay in that area and continue to accept this way of life.

I returned home from my two-day fact finding excursion on a Saturday afternoon and by the following Tuesday morning the company had put an offer on the table. And it wasn't a bad offer at that. Not great, mind you, but not bad either, especially for the south. The big ticket item of the offer was a duel package relocation assistance plan that included both full reimbursement for all moving expenses as well as company paid temporary housing for up to 60 days while we searched for a permanent place to live. There was also going to be a two-week, company paid PLC training program available to all new maintenance employees that I really wanted to attend.

The pay? Well that could have been better; $13.00 per hour to start was what they were offering. Not quite what I was hoping for. Actually, it was amazingly low by industrial maintenance standards. But it wasn't bad for the south. And it beat anything I was ever offered in Myrtle Beach by far.

I discussed the pay scale with the maintenance manager during my interview and he told me the range was from $10.00 to $19.00 per hour for maintenance people. I was hoping to hit somewhere closer to the upper end of that scale, but in reality, I was anticipating an offer closer to the middle. Although I did have a minor electronics background, all my industrial maintenance experience was mechanical, and most companies pay more for electrical skills than mechanical. So although I would have liked more by the hour, I thought their total offer including the relocation package was generous.

I phoned the personnel manager and told him I was giving their offer serious consideration and would make a decision within the next two days. Shortly after hanging up with him, I received a call from the maintenance manager. He told me most of the new equipment going into this plant was manufactured by a company in Holland and a group from the plant was going there for a two-week training session. Then he played his trump card. He told me if I accepted their offer, I would be one of the employees going on this trip. He also told me if I accepted their offer and got there in three weeks, I would lock myself into a guaranteed first shift position. Being a family man, this was extremely important to me. At least half of the shifts on average I was working on the casino boat were night shifts. And I hated every last minute of it.

I phoned my wife at work to fill her in on the latest developments. The personnel manager had originally told me they had dozens more candidates to interview and it would take at least two weeks to make a final decision on most employment offers, but I was a strong candidate. On our way back to Myrtle Beach, my wife and I agreed we would want to make at least one more trip back to Georgia before considering such a major move. So this sudden quick decision was one we would have preferred not to be thrust into. But after a few minutes of discussion, we decided this very well could be a once-in-a-lifetime opportunity. It had become obvious that relocating to Myrtle Beach was a mistake that was going to cause us to live paycheck to paycheck for the rest of our lives with no opportunity for retirement. And this was a paid ticket out. So with her blessing, I made a phone call with my official acceptance.

The maintenance manager phoned me again shortly afterwards. He informed me that upper management had some reservations about sending a new employee on the training trip to Holland. They were concerned I might accept the job just to get the trip to Holland and leave the company shortly after, without them receiving any return for their investment in me. So to counter their concerns, he asked if I would be willing to sign a statement guaranteeing I would reimburse the company for my travel expenses if I left their employment on my own accord within a year. The decision to sign was a no-brainer as far as I was concerned. Why would I even consider uprooting my family and moving over 200 miles away to a place I knew absolutely no one to take a job for less than a year? So he faxed me a copy of the agreement. I signed it, faxed it back, and the deal was sealed.

I arrived in Georgia three weeks later for my first day of work. The cook plant section of the facility I was hired for was nowhere close to being up and running and we were scheduled to leave for Holland on Friday, so I wasn't anticipating a busy first week. I was the sixth man hired for the maintenance crew. The first man hired was on temporary assignment in the existing facility. Two others were back in North and South Carolina, preparing for their final moves to Georgia after securing permanent housing. So my first day's assignment was a simple one. I met two of my new coworkers and they were instructed to show me around.

The rest of the week was pretty much more of the same. We were instructed to just put in our eight hours so we would get a full week's pay and learn what we could about the facility. The place was still in the preliminary construction phase so there wasn't a lot we could do. Much of the equipment hadn't even been delivered yet, and what was there wasn't hooked up. So it wasn't like we could walk around and test run machines. We spent four days wandering around a construction zone, trying to familiarize ourselves with the layout of the facility and learn what we could about the plant's infrastructure. We spent time in the attic, up on the roof, and in any nook or cranny we thought might be an area we needed to be familiar with when the time came for us to take responsibility for keeping this entire facility up and running.

During this time, I dropped into the personnel manager's office to thank him again for the opportunity, not only for the job, but also for the training in Holland. He confided in me that there were four new people they considered key to the success of this plant's start-up. The first was the maintenance manager responsible for hiring me, who was brought in just a few months earlier and was hired specifically to recruit a crew of experienced maintenance personnel for this start-up. I was also considered one of the four key individuals due to my 22 years of experience in food manufacturing and my spotless work record. The other two key individuals were an industrial electrician and an installation engineer, both hired away from a major-brand-name baked products plant in the Raleigh, North Carolina area. So it wasn't just a coincidence that the four of us were the four selected to attend the training in Holland. And it was also not just me, but all four of us that were required to sign the agreement to repay travel expenses clause should we quit within a year. Perhaps I should have seen a red flag and wondered why they were so concerned with locking us all in. But I didn't read it that way. If anything, I took it as a compliment. This company was not only willing to spend thousands of dollars to recruit, relocate and train me, but they were also concerned with keeping me around. This was something I was no longer accustomed to after spending almost six years in the Myrtle Beach job market where the philosophy always has been "the one who is willing to work the cheapest is automatically the most qualified," and they'll fire you in a heartbeat if they think they can replace you with someone for a nickel per hour less.

Thursday rolled around and the three of us going on the Holland trip were called to the maintenance manager's office shortly after lunch. We briefly went over our itinerary and finalized arrangements for transportation to the airport in the morning. We were then each handed a $500 check to cover miscellaneous expenses and were given an hour off to go to town and cash the checks. I was on Cloud 9. This was the type of opportunity I was hoping for all my life. Keith, one of the other new hires fortunate enough to be selected to go on this training trip, coined the phrase "we all hit a home run" earlier in the week when we were discussing the opportunities that could be associated with getting in on the ground floor on such a major expansion. And this just confirmed his sentiments in my mind.

We arrived in Holland on a Saturday morning but training didn't start until Monday, so we had a full weekend off. The company we were training at was actually in the heart of nowhere in a small town. But the company had arranged for us to spend the weekend in Amsterdam and be transported out to where we were being trained Sunday evening. So, the four of us spent the weekend together, kicking around Amsterdam, getting to know one another, discussing our new employer and generally just having a real good time.

My new employer couldn't have made a better first impression on me. I had been privileged to take a few trips with my original employer after achieving a leadership position. The accommodations and other perks were always well above what I was used to experiencing in my personal traveling experiences, but they were nothing compared to what I was experiencing now. This was first class all the way. This was a company I couldn't wait to start busting my ass for.

After returning from Holland, we spent a couple of weeks hanging around with the vendors installing a spiral freezer. Then it was off to the local tech school for a two-week PLC training program. Shortly after that program was over, we took a week long road trip to a poultry plant in South Carolina that we were going to be doing some co-packing for. During these following weeks, a few more new hires were thrown into the mix and collectively, we made one hell of a team. If there ever was such a thing as a maintenance dream team, this was it. To start, there were my Holland travel buddies, Fred and Keith. Fred was a 30-year plus industrial electrician veteran with an AA degree in electrical engineering. There wasn't anything with wires or electronics that Fred didn't understand. Keith was an all around mechanical/electrical whiz kid. He had worked for years as an industrial welder before becoming an installation engineer. Then there was James. He just came out of a nine year stint with the Navy where he was an electronics instructor. James had no manufacturing experience, but like Fred, there wasn't anything electrical or electronic that could stump him. Dave was the mechanical guru of the bunch. He had five years maintenance experience under his belt in a major soft drink manufacturing facility and worked several years before that with an aircraft manufacturer. Dave was a welder, fabricator, heavy equipment operator and hydraulics specialist, in addition to being a top-notch mechanic. He also had basic electrical skills. Jake went to work for a Chicago-based construction firm shortly after high school where he installed motorized conveyor systems in manufacturing facilities all across the country. He wasn't Fred or James, but he still had good electrical skills and was also very strong mechanically. Mike had just been laid off from a position as an Electro/mechanical maintenance technician with a Fortune 500 candy manufacturer. Like Fred, Keith, Dave and myself, Mike had decades of experience in manufacturing. Collectively, we literally had over a hundred years of experience in food manufacturing in mostly Fortune 500 facilities and came from three different states.

Then there were the local guys. They were much younger than us manufacturing dinosaurs. But they were full of potential. Justin was hired away from a local sawmill. He had an AA in electronics and a little over a year of experience as an electrician in the mill. Roy was an electronics whiz kid. Like James, Roy had never seen the inside of a manufacturing facility. But at about 23 or 24 years old, he knew more about electronics and technology than many technicians twice his age. Another young local was Bill. He had some kind of electrical certificate from the local tech school and had been running his own business installing auto stereo systems. He had never seen the inside of a factory, and didn't have a lot of built-in mechanical ability. But he was definitely teachable. The last one hired was a young local named Josh. Josh was straight out of high school. He actually had to spend his first couple of months with the company working in the stockroom until his 18th birthday when he was finally old enough to work on the factory floor. He actually attended a tech school while still in high school and received his electrical certificate and high school diploma at the same time. He was possibly the smartest 18-year-old kid I ever met. Collectively, we were ready to take this place by storm.

Chapter 12. Dream Team Turns Nightmare

It became apparent early on there were reasons far beyond just low wages this company couldn't get local residents to accept jobs in this facility. The working conditions certainly didn't add any extra incentive. Temperature extremes of hot and cold, raw meat, wet floors and foul odors all added to the undesirability of this facility. But those were all minor compared to the biggest undesirable trait this plant had, a mean-spirited management staff that only knew motivation through threats and intimidation. That may have worked with the unskilled types doing the routine floor jobs, especially the illegal ones that were afraid of their own shadows. But for anyone who had confidence in their own personal value to an employer, a little respect didn't seem like too much to ask.

Shortly after Justin was hired, the saw mill he left to take this position started calling him in an effort to reverse recruit him back into their fold. Before resorting to offering more money to accomplish this task, they started by using the company's bad reputation in an attempt to lure Justin away. Justin quickly gained the confidence of some of the maintenance crew in the existing facility and was shocked when his new friends pretty much verified all the allegations his old employer was making about his new employer's local reputation for extremely long hours, miserable working conditions, tyrannical management procedures and unsafe work practices. So, shortly after we returned to the plant from our two week PLC training program at the local tech school, Justin went out for lunch leaving a note behind for the maintenance manager, and none of us ever saw him again. Perhaps this should have served as an early warning to upper management that highly experienced and heavily recruited candidates required a little more special handling than the non-English speaking, unskilled, illegal workforce they were accustomed to dealing with. But it didn't. If anything, they got meaner.

Things got crazy quickly. The construction of the new facility was way behind schedule and everyone was in panic mode. Office politics obviously ruled and most of management seemed intertwined in a vicious round of finger-pointing and playing the blame game. One thing became obvious quickly; management couldn't stand to see anyone stand still for even a split second. We were expected to be going a 100 miles per hour the entire time we were on the clock. Biggest problem with this theory was we had almost nothing to do. The place was still a construction zone and we had no real set assignments. We were instructed by our manager to find something to do or stay out of site.

The latter wasn't nearly as easy as it may sound, however, due to the layout of the plant. The production area was a long narrow straight line. The office area was on the second floor of the East wall running almost the full length of the production area. The hallway, along with the plant manager's office, was lined with large windows that always had countless managers leaning against the glass peering down onto the production floor.

Anytime two or more people were seen standing and talking, you could see the big-wigs up in the window whipping out their cell phones. A few moments later we'd get the call over the radio asking what we were doing. It didn't matter if we said we were discussing something regarding the facility, we would be told to get our asses moving and find something constructive to do.

After several weeks of wandering around aimlessly, trying to stay away from one another and look busy with no actual work assignments in a small and closely monitored facility, somebody finally actually used their head and decided we could be utilized to do some of the work the company was paying contractors to do, thus keeping us busy while saving the company some money in contractor's fees. Most of us were actually thrilled at the concept of having something to do. It's not like we wanted to wander around all day and do nothing. It was quite boring, not to mention frustrating. If I was told one more time to "get my ass busy" then told to "find something" when I asked what I should get busy doing, I think I would have screamed.

Once we officially became part of the construction process, however, we found out quickly why this whole process was so far behind schedule. We would spend an entire morning lining up a piece of equipment, making sure it was located exactly where the blueprint showed it, and making even more so sure it was perfectly square before bolting it down to the floor after all being excoriated because the first piece we installed was found to be approximately a quarter of an inch out of square. Then we would come in the following morning and be instructed to grind off the bolts and move the same piece of equipment we had so painstakingly positioned perfectly the day before two-feet over or two-inches forward according to an updated print. This went on for weeks and we all found ourselves quickly losing faith in the decision making of our upper management staff. How could they be complaining that the entire project was so far behind schedule (not to mention constantly trying to find someone to blame it on) when they still were not even sure what it was they wanted? The layout of the plant would change sometimes as much as two or three times in a day. It was a constant game of hurry up and bolt that down over there, then, oh wait a minute, grind off those bolt heads and bring it over here. A barely walked on floor began to look like it was 20-years-old in a matter of months.

The man originally hired to be our plant manager obviously recognized a three-ring circus when he saw one because he quit and headed back to the Midwest before the construction phase of the plant was even close to finished. Little did we know it at the time, but that was the first of dozens of upper management figures that would come and go before this place even came close to celebrating its first anniversary.

As time went on the insanity not only continued, but worsened. We all felt like we were under a microscope. Our skill levels, commitment and even our work ethics were questioned and challenged every day. This was a company that had spent months of time in recruiting and thousands of dollars per person in relocation expenses to bring us here and now it almost seemed as if they wanted us to fail.

Mike was the first to feel the sting from this management's wrath. Back in the days when we were still a construction zone and had almost nothing constructive to do anyway, he requested to leave a couple of hours early on his daughter's birthday. It didn't seem like such an unreasonable request. After all, his whole family was crammed into a hotel room hundreds of miles away from anyone they knew while they were going through the relocation process. They were making a huge sacrifice for him to take a job with this company. And all he wanted was a couple of extra hours to show his appreciation back to them for their support, on his daughter's birthday no less. And this was on a day when we were doing nothing in particular at the plant to top it off. So it should have been a win, win situation. Mike could have spent some extra time with his family on his daughter's birthday and the company could have saved a couple of hours of pay for a maintenance tech that wasn't doing anything productive that day anyway.

But his request was promptly denied. The maintenance manager said he didn't want to set a precedent that would give his maintenance crew the idea we could leave early anytime we asked. A sound business practice in the real world, perhaps, but in this temporary situation we were in where the company was basically paying us many times to be on site and do nothing because the start up of the new facility was so far behind schedule, this would have been the most logical time to grant requests for time off. We all knew time off would be almost impossible to get once we started production, so why not give us a break now? Not to mention it wasn't like we were a bunch of teenagers on our first jobs that needed to be broken in properly from the start. The majority of us were in our late-30s to mid-40s with 20-plus years of experience under our belts. We knew what an employer expected out of us and were more than ready to deliver.

A few weeks later when Mike needed a Monday off so he could take a long weekend to return to Tennessee and tie up some loose ends, he did what the majority of people in his situation would do. He lied. After all, he tried the truth the first time around and that didn't work out very well. So he left for Tennessee that Friday afternoon and called in sick Monday. Apparently, he was still in Tennessee when he made the call Monday morning. And apparently the company monitored incoming calls because somehow they knew he had called from Tennessee.

So when he returned to work on Tuesday he was called into the maintenance manager's office for a severe tongue lashing along with a promise of termination if he ever did anything like that again. Well apparently Mike knew something this company didn't. If they were willing to pay to relocate him due to his experience, so would someone else. Within a matter of weeks after this incident, Mike found a company in his home state willing to pay his way back home in exchange for his services and our highly recruited department suffered its second casualty.

Apparently, the company was not happy about someone they invested that kind of money in quitting before they had a chance to fire him. And they displayed their frustration by refusing to give him his last check. They said they were holding his last check to recoup some of the hotel expenses the company had spent to house him and his family while he was working there. And they made sure we all knew about it. I found that strange in itself. There was zero communication between management and employees at this company, except, of course, when they were screaming and swearing at us over the radio. But this was made known throughout the whole department. Intended as a warning to the rest of us that if we tried to quit after they spent so much money to get us there, they would find a way to make us regret it, no doubt.

And so the saga continued. Keith was appointed our lead man and his first rule of thumb with this company became, "if you don't know something, don't admit it." That was another managerial philosophy I just didn't get. During my days as a team leader, I encouraged people to come to me if they didn't understand something. How else would I be able to help them if I didn't know they were struggling with something? Not to mention creating an atmosphere where people felt they had to hide inexperience or misunderstanding was a recipe for disaster and a good way to get people hurt. But this place had turned into a jungle, and as I realized later, probably always had been. It was survival of the fittest and admitting you didn't know something would lead to certain death at the hands of a mean-spirited management staff that was looking to blame the delayed start-up of this plant on anyone and everyone they could.

Tensions were brewing daily, and I knew by the time start-up actually arrived, things would be ugly. Management had already set up an "us versus them" mentality before the first pound of chicken was even cooked. And I knew that philosophy would equate to disaster in a stressful start-up situation. What started out as a maintenance dream team was quickly turning into a relocation nightmare. Many of our highly recruited members were already looking for new jobs before we even started up. They had the sense to realize if it was this bad now; it would only get worse when the ovens started rolling.

And when the ovens did start rolling, the three-ring-circus expanded. Everything was basically turned on full speed, with little to no trial runs or break-in periods, and management expected to be operating in the black during the plant's first week. When we were still not out of the red in our second week of production, our maintenance manager, the man most responsible for bringing us all here, was held accountable for the inevitable failure of the miserably planned and totally unprepared plant start-up and lost his job.

Personally, I always found that just a little bit odd. We went into production totally unprepared with a plant manager that was actually hired as an assistant and was thrown in the job unexpectedly when our original plant manager resigned, a largely untrained and unskilled production crew, most of whom couldn't even speak English, in a facility designed by an engineering group that consisted of two engineers that were changing designs all the way up until--and beyond—the day before start-up, yet somehow it was the maintenance manager, the only person who showed any real advanced preparation and planning within his area of responsibility, that got hit with the full blame for the failed start-up.

Although I don't believe it was ever made official, Keith became our new fearless leader. We all initially breathed a deep sigh of relief figuring we had one of our own now in a position where he could go to bat for us. That was something we really needed because everything was written off on the back of the maintenance department. When the entire upper level conveyor system failed to operate properly, it was somehow the maintenance department's fault. Even though we initially tried to warn management we found major glitches and conflicts in the system's logic when we managed to sneak over and try it out after management was informed by the installation contractors and the vendor's field engineer that the system was fully operational and management signed off on the project without heeding our warnings. When the spiral freezer failed to properly reach operating temperature inside the spiral because the removable panels had been bent out of shape beyond repair by careless sanitation workers dropping them on the ground from the second tier catwalk, it was somehow the maintenance department's fault. When the rebuilt and guaranteed to be good as new manual sealers the company purchased from a used food equipment vendor, that we were never given a chance to test—or even see, for that fact—before the first day we put them into operation failed, it was somehow the maintenance department's fault. When we eventually got the "used but rebuilt and good as new" manual sealers operating at an almost acceptable level and couldn't seal bags because we were trying to force 10-pounds of chicken into the five-pound bags ordered by management, it was somehow the maintenance department's fault.

But Keith wasn't nearly the ally we had hoped for. He tried. He really did. But he was caught in a crossfire between maintenance men he knew were more than capable of collectively doing the job at hand but expected to be treated with the respect and appreciation our collective skills and experience deserved and an upper management whose philosophy was motivation through fear and intimidation.

Months after production had finally started management was still trying to change the design of the plant. The plan this particular day was after running a full day of production (which usually took about 12 to 13 hours) maintenance was to install a new injector on the line after production was finished for the day. The one flaw with this plan was there was only one full shift of maintenance men at that time with a couple of guys working staggered shifts to provide minimal coverage after production hours and during sanitation time. So this meant the same people who had been working since 6:00 in the morning would be required to stay on the clock until production was finished and the new injector install was completed.

When 8:00 in the evening rolled around and most of the maintenance staff had been on the clock for 14 hours, the installation project seemed to be stalled and going nowhere fast due to the fact that management had the entire maintenance department in a holding pattern, awaiting further instruction as to exactly how they wanted the injector installed. And no one in charge seemed to be showing any sense of urgency as to getting this project started so maintenance could get done and go home. Dave took it upon himself to go see the higher-ups and find out why.

Dave was the classic all-American biker type and was anything but timid. Apparently, when Dave didn't get the answers he was looking for in regard to why no one in management was showing any urgency to get the maintenance crew the resources they needed to get the job started, things got heated. And when the discussion was over, Dave was told since he seemed so unhappy with the way management handled things in this facility he could go home and not bother to come back.

Diplomacy was not Dave's strongest personal trait. Confrontational would probably sum that one up better. So I'm sure he didn't handle the situation as tactfully as he should. As a matter of fact, I'd be willing to bet he exploded into the office like a storm trooper and thoroughly irritated everyone.

But even so, he had a legitimate complaint. As a team leader at my original employer, I probably would have been fired for forcing someone to work over 14 hours against their will. But here, people got fired for complaining about having to work over 14 hours.

Then came the plight of Keith. I don't know if he was ever officially coined "maintenance manger" but he was doing his damndest to fill the gap ever since our original manager's departure nonetheless. He was the first one there and the last one to leave almost every day; going 100 miles per hour in every direction he could the whole time. And how was he rewarded? He was told to come to work at 5:00 in the morning just so they could tell him to turn around and go home because his services were no longer required. And this was done on a Saturday morning, no less. They couldn't have told him at the end of the day Friday?

Personally, I think the whole thing was orchestrated by the new plant manager to save his own butt. He was the third plant manager to this point that couldn't get this place up and running properly and needed a fall guy to blame it on. This ploy didn't buy him much time, however. Within a couple of months after Keith's exit, he was demoted to manager of the dreaded evisceration department. Rumor had it that was the fate for management types the company really had an axe to grind with and wanted to humiliate instead of simply terminate.

It wasn't long after this that Roy and Josh quit almost simultaneously. In addition to all the standard complaints the rest of maintenance had both Roy and Josh were also not happy about being forced onto second shift after being promised first shift positions. So within six-months of the exhausting efforts this company made to recruit such a high quality maintenance team our crew of 10 was down to five, with none of the remaining five feeling very much loyalty to this company.

James had originally been put in charge of the second shift crew when it was created and when Keith was let go, he became the official first shift maintenance supervisor. His first order of business was to attempt to replenish the dwindling maintenance department with some new blood, a task that would not be easy. One of the owners directly responsible for the cook plant start-up had previously made the statement that the company would no longer recruit out of state candidates and would also never again use a head hunter. It was obvious recruiting and relocating maintenance people with experience from real "World Class" companies was not a viable option because this company couldn't—or at least wouldn't—match the working climate these highly desirable candidates were accustomed to. It takes a lot more to be a "World Class" facility than simply deciding to call yourself one. And as far as the head hunter issue was concerned, the rumor on the production floor from the small handful of "employee friendly" supervisors that actually talked to us when they didn't have something to scream about was that virtually every reputable recruiter in the business had black-balled the company due to all the negative feedback received back from management employees sent to the company by recruiters.

James managed to find four or five local candidates to fill the slots opened by the untimely exits of our counterparts. One worked out well and became a permanent and useful member of the department. Another one actually quit before lunch rolled around on his first day. The rest all quit within a matter of a few weeks. So now we were six, one new, four disgruntled (included in that four was James who was trying to play the dual role of boss and coworker and was no happier with the over-demanding management staff than the rest of us) and one in total shut down. And unfortunately for the company, the one in shut down was Fred, who just happened to also be our most knowledgeable and experienced maintenance employee, not to mention our only true electrician left other than James. Like Roy and Josh, Fred was also forced onto second shift against his will after being promised a first shift position and was no happier about it than they were. Unlike the other two, however, Fred had locked himself into this company for a year with the same Holland travel expense agreement I had hanging over my head. So he did not have the option of showing his dissatisfaction by quitting like Roy and Josh did. At least, not without suffering a large financial setback that is. But Fred was a loophole kind of guy. And he found himself one heck of a loophole. The agreement clearly stated he would be responsible for reimbursing the company for his traveling expenses to Holland if he left the company on his own accord within a year. But nowhere did the agreement state anything about him being required to put forth any genuine effort during that year. So he didn't. He was late almost every day, he left whenever he decided he was ready to go home without checking with—or even informing—anyone from management and he did as little as possible in between those two times.

I didn't agree with the game Fred was playing. But I certainly did understand it. We all react to situations differently. And this was Fred's way of bearing with an almost unbearable situation. Many successful companies would be considered "tough" in the way they deal with their employees. A no nonsense approach could be another way of stating that. And there really isn't anything wrong with that in itself if that approach works for a particular company. But this went so far past anything even remotely close to what should be considered "acceptable" management policies, tough or otherwise. This company was downright mean. Humiliating, demeaning and intimidating employees were standard operating procedures. Management demanded the impossible, expected the improbable and showed zero respect or appreciation for anyone on the work room floor. Sometimes I think management believed their tongues would be cut out if they ever said something like "thank you" or "good job" to an employee. There was no such thing as words of encouragement or praise for employees at this company, just criticism, anger and dissention. Secretly, I don't believe any of us wanted to see this company succeed due to the resentment we all harbored brought on by the abusive management policies this company employed. Fred was just the only one defiant enough to outwardly display the anger we were all carrying inside.

If this department, and ultimately this new facility, were to survive, someone had to stop the bleeding. A new personnel manager was hired and James seized the opportunity to campaign for help to resolve our department's turnover woes. The new manager asked James what he thought would be needed to improve morale and reduce turnover. James told him he thought we needed more money and better treatment. Surprising, after reviewing our recent turnover record, the new manager agreed.

I didn't know exactly how much anyone else's raise was, nor did I care. All I knew for sure was I got two bucks and just like that I jumped from $13.00 to $15.00 per hour. That was a badly needed morale booster.

James also secured a promise of more money for Roy and Josh as well if they were willing to come back. Josh accepted with the condition he was also put back on first shift. Roy never returned James's call.

The ironic part about all this is, by the time the company realized the importance of retaining talented maintenance people, some of the most talented were already gone. And the majority of the rest had at least one foot pointed towards the door. Keith, Mike and Justin were all excellent electricians, something we were now experiencing a terrible shortage of. Roy was also a brilliant electronic technician with strong electrical skills. Not to mention at his young age, someone with a lifetime of potential ahead of him. And Dave was without a doubt our strongest mechanical asset. But they were all gone and finding suitable replacements was beginning to seem impossible.

This sudden show of appreciation also came too late for Jake. He gladly accepted his pay increase. But he had been talking to other companies all over the country for months and had several tentative offers in the works. It wasn't long after these pay increases went into effect before he was off to Minnesota for a 20 plus dollar per hour job. This was another big loss for the company. Jake didn't posses the superior electrical skills of James or Fred but he was still one of our stronger electronic technician types and was also very proficient mechanically. And perhaps even more importantly, he was aggressive when it came to getting involved in troubleshooting, wasn't afraid to take charge of a situation when someone needed to and almost certainly would have become a future leader in this company had he stayed.

Fred's raise, I later learned, was 25¢ per hour. James had tried to get him more based on his experience. But management said he was lucky to get the quarter because they didn't like his attitude. That didn't surprise any of us. Most of Fred's coworkers didn't like his attitude either. But for a large part, management created that attitude. Fred was one of the most intelligent people I ever met. And he was the most proficient electrician I ever worked with. Additionally, he was also an amazing electronics technician. Computers, networking, fiber optics, AC drives, PLC programming, you name it. If it was electronic, Fred knew it. Another thing Fred knew was his value to an employer. And he was not going to allow this management staff, or any other, to treat him like a second-class citizen. He knew he deserved better. And the management staff should have as well. Electricians of his caliber were not easy to find. But this company was nondiscriminatory to the core. They treated everyone exactly the same regardless of experience or talent—badly. Extremely badly!

There were many events that led up to Fred's highly detested attitude, I'm sure. But there was one in particular I remember that I believe was key. The spiral freezer went down. No rhyme. No reason. It just suddenly stopped for no apparent cause. Management immediately panicked, as they always did—yelling, screaming, swearing, threatening to send people home if the line was not back up and running immediately, which then threw maintenance into a panic. All except for Fred, that is. Fred never panicked. That in itself was enough to infuriate this management staff. Every situation, no matter how minor or how routine, was a major disaster in the eyes of our overbearing management staff. And they expected to see everyone involved display their same panicked reaction. But Fred was too confident in his abilities to panic. And rightfully so because he knew no matter what the problem was, he was capable of correcting it.

So while everyone else was running around in panic mode trying to guess their way through the problem, Fred was doing what skilled electricians do. He pulled out the operations manual and was studying the schematic for the freezer's electrical panel as part of his troubleshooting preparation when an overzealous manager gets on the radio for all to hear and starts screaming, "The line's down and Fred Smith is standing around reading a book!"

To which Fred took great offense. In that brief moment in time, with a stupid statement blurted out by an incompetent manager, Fred crossed the line from disgruntled employee to dissatisfied employee. And once there, he was never coming back.

Shortly after we all received our pay increases, the man we had to thank for them, James, turned in his resignation. He couldn't take the constant hounding of upper management any longer. James may have come through with the more money part but the better treatment he also campaigned for never materialized. The last thing he said to me before leaving was, "Hey, at least I was the first one in charge of this department that managed to quit before they could fire me."

CHAPTER 13. WHEN ALL ELSE FAILS, GET MEANER

Just when we thought things couldn't get any worse, upper management decided it was time for yet another major shake-up. Enter The Intimidator. Our fourth plant manager in less than a year barely had his feet on the floor and upper management again decided he wasn't delivering the proper results. But with less than two months under his belt, instead of firing or demoting him to a humiliating position like evisceration, they allowed him to keep his position but made The Intimidator, a very unpopular manager from the antiquated old facility the top gun over both facilities. And The Intimidator made his presence known immediately.

This place was already without a doubt more miserable than most people could even imagine, but The Intimidator somehow managed to ratchet up the misery index exponentially on a daily basis. He was meaner, more impatient, more threatening, more demanding, more condescending, and more insulting than any before him. And that was saying something because there were some first class son-of-a-bitches in this company's fast growing management hall of shame.

The first policy change implemented under this regime was targeted directly at the maintenance department. Right after James succeeded in increasing wages in an attempt to improve morale in our plagued department and reduce turnover, The Intimidator decided our department was overpaid. Under the new policy, all newly hired maintenance technicians started out at a maximum of $10.00 per hour. As if we weren't having a hard enough time staffing the maintenance department as it was, the quality of our new hires really dropped dramatically with this new starting wage. From that day forward the average age of a new hire for the maintenance department was around 20 to 22, mostly local farm kids that had never before seen the inside of a manufacturing facility and had no industrial electricity experience. But they were expected to work in 480-volt electrical panels just like the rest of us. All maintenance technicians were created equal at this company. And we were all expected to perform the same mechanical, electrical and electronic duties, fully qualified or not.

I wasn't qualified to work in 480-volt electrical panels. And I certainly wasn't an electrician. All my maintenance experience at the first plant I worked in was strictly mechanical and electrically I was at best a low-voltage electronic technician due to my experience with the cable manufacturer and my short stint repairing slot machines. And my resume clearly reflected those facts. But with Fred now on second shift and James gone, I was the closest thing to an electrician in the packaging area on first shift and had no choice but to pretend to be one. And that was a scary scenario.

Fortunately, I was resourceful and a fairly quick learner. I figured out early on I was going to be expected to do things at this company I wasn't qualified to do. So I immediately latched on to guys like Keith, Fred, James and Mike. I followed them around like a little lost puppy and learned everything I could from them all in the few months I had to work with them. And thankfully, between what I picked up from them, combined with the little I knew on my own from my basic electronics courses I took while working for the cable manufacturer, I was able to get in and out of 480-volt electrical panels on a daily basis and somehow managed not to electrocute myself, in spite of the fact that I wasn't an electrician.

But now I had people around me going in and out of these panels everyday that knew even less than me about higher voltage electricity. With most of them knowing a lot less than me. Now that was a really scary scenario! And somehow I felt like their ultimate safety was somehow my responsibility. I guess it had something to do with being the senior maintenance tech on the entire shift after approximately six months.

At the original plant I worked in we had packaging mechanics, electricians, PLC specialists, mobile equipment mechanics, machinists and stationary engineers. All of which operated within their own area of expertise—and only in their area of expertise—after extensive training to become specialists. And all of these "specialists" were compensated anywhere from $19.00 per hour for a low level mechanic to well over $20.00 per hour for machinists, electricians and electronics specialists. At this company a "maintenance technician" was expected to be able to do "all of the above" as well as jobs normally associated with production workers such as set-up and basic operation. Our original crew was expected to do all of this for the $13.00 to $14.00 per hour range. And new hires were now expected to do all these duties that normally command a

$20.00+ per hour rate per position for a ridiculous $10.00 per hour for the entire package. Yet upper management couldn't understand why they were having such difficulty finding and retaining qualified maintenance people.

As we struggled to keep the plant running with a bunch of here today, gone tomorrow, young and inexperienced $10.00 per hour maintenance techs, The Intimidator's tirades of terror continued. He would come crashing through the door like a Nazi storm trooper, yelling, screaming, nitpicking every little piece of the operation apart. He would find any simple reason to shut down the line then bitch, moan and threaten because production time was being lost. Sometimes I think it was nothing more than a big game to him, nothing more than a major power trip. I think he derived some kind of erotic pleasure from seeing people nervous, frustrated and intimidated.

One of his favorite games to play during one-shift operations was to stroll in around 6:00 or 7:00 at night (after most of the room had been on the clock for 12 hours or more and we were nearing the end of the production run and could soon go home) and he would order the line to be shut down. He would then leave a laundry list with the supervisors in charge of problems that had to be corrected before the line could be restarted. He would then leave shortly afterwards, knowing damn well he just caused everyone else to be doomed to somewhere around a 15 or 16 hour shift that wouldn't end until somewhere around 10:00 or 11:00 at night and then expect everyone back at 6:00 in the morning the next day.

He essentially cost the company thousands of dollars in unnecessary overtime and set up a potentially dangerous situation, by forcing an entire crew to work well over what should be considered a normal shift. Not to mention risked not having a full crew for start up in the morning and thoroughly pissed everyone off. And for what? To show everyone who was in charge?

The Intimidator's reign of terror continued daily. One day the plant manager, having had his fill of The Intimidator's demeaning, condescending and humiliating production floor manner, walked off the job. Never would I ever have thought someone in such a prestigious position could be rattled to the point of walking off the job. But that was the misery index The Intimidator was capable of delivering. And again, the company wondered why they couldn't keep reliable help. If a plant manager couldn't take this misery, why would anyone in a lower position?

I was certain The Intimidator's days were numbered at that point. After all, how long would upper management tolerate someone running off plant managers? Much longer then I realized, apparently, because that plant manager's exit was followed by countless supervisors, managers, and shift coordinators, all of which threw their arms up in the middle of a shift and walked out based on something said directly by The Intimidator and/or his Nazi-style cronies.

Less than a year after production started upper management decided they weren't happy with the performance of their new facility and shut it down for a major facelift. This was a scary proposition for a couple of reasons. The most obvious being another start-up of new equipment under the same conditions as the first time would undoubtedly produce the same disastrous results. After all, this wasn't a company that seemed to learn from their past mistakes. They just continued to make the same ones over and over again while finding new people to blame them on each time. And with The Intimidator's reign of terror still in full swing, the slightest miscue would no doubt result in severe consequences.

But before making it to another failed start-up attempt, we first had to weather another construction zone storm. Which meant we would all again be challenged with light work schedules in a facility where being seen standing idle for even a minute could get you terminated. We were all called in for a meeting and warned in no uncertain terms we had to find a way to stay busy at all times throughout the entire construction process if we hoped to see the second start-up. Our manager knew Fred would never conform to these guidelines. So he decided to save Fred from himself and transferred him to evisceration for the duration of the reconstruction.

Why Fred was never fired remains a mystery. This company loved to fire people. Setting an example for others is probably the way they would describe it. And they fired many a people for far less than some of the things Fred got away with on a daily basis. Perhaps contrary to what they displayed outwardly, they really did appreciate Fred's skills and experience and realized they needed to keep him around for the times when no one else knew the answer. Maybe they hoped he would eventually come around and be the productive employee everyone knew he was capable of being. If I had to guess, my opinion would be they thought Fred wanted to be fired because he knew he couldn't quit without suffering a heavy financial consequence due to the Holland travel agreement he signed. And this company seemed to derive great pleasure from making sure people didn't get what they wanted.

Fred did eventually quit. Exactly one year and a day after the four of us penned our names to the travel agreements that locked us into this dreaded company for a year unless we were willing to eat the travel expenses for Holland, the grand total for which was never even revealed to us. Fred came to see me on his last day. His spiel went something like this: "Hey Clyde. I just wanted to let you know I just told our boss I was turning in my two-day notice. He looked at me and said, 'You're only giving me a two-day notice?' So I looked him square in the eye and said,

'That's right, I quit—Today!' Then the dumb ass asked me if I was going to finish the shift. So I looked him square in the eye again and said, 'You don't get this, do you? I'm giving you a today notice, I quit—today.' Well Clyde, it's been nice working with you. I'll see you around."

And out the door walked the facility's only true electrician. I must admit, I was more than just a little jealous. I wanted to go out the door with him so badly. But by the same token, this was the fourth job I had in less than seven years. So I was bound and determined to make sure the next one was the right one. Perhaps the most impressive overall attribute on my resume was my 22 years on my first job. But that stability was starting to look like a fluke with the way short-lived careers were starting to stack up underneath it. So I decided I had no real choice except to stick it out until a real opportunity came along.

It wasn't like I hadn't been looking for other opportunities as that long awaited one year Anniversary approached. Keith had secured a maintenance position with a local glass manufacturer shortly after his unexpected exit from this company. He was extremely happy there and managed to get me an interview with the maintenance manager. The interview went well and the manager put me on a waiting list. Unfortunately, there were already two other experienced candidates on that list ahead of me. So the big question became, how long would I have to wait?

And long before that, Mike was trying to lure me to Tennessee to come to work for his new employer. But I had already ripped my wife and daughter away from everyone they knew and brought them to an unfamiliar place once. And there was no way I was going to put them through that again in less than a year.

So while Fred strolled off into the sunset with a big smile on his face, I prepared to go through another start-up, with a man in charge that was probably at least as mean and vindictive as all the others before him combined. The two young locals, Bill and Josh, were the only other remaining techs from the original start-up crew besides me. The rest of the maintenance crew had no idea just what a rough road lay ahead of them.

Chapter 14. Insanity: Take Two

The first couple of weeks of this abrupt shutdown weren't really that bad. It was easy enough to remain busy and stay out of trouble. We were virtually tearing the place apart from top to bottom. And I must admit, I really did enjoy ripping out some of the troublesome equipment that was never installed properly to begin with and made my life hell from day one.

But as the initial "tear apart" began winding down, meaningful work again became scarce. And The Intimidator and his cronies were on the prowl, just waiting to pounce on anyone seen idle for even a minute. Most companies in this position would resort to temporary lay-offs until the facility was back up and running. But that never seemed to be a serious consideration here. My guess is the company realized if they laid people off, essentially giving them an opportunity to go into a full time job search, they would never see them again. Yet they seemed to have no problem with firing people for any trivial little thing.

Up until now, we had used the original facility's maintenance supply for general supplies. Parts that were specifically for our equipment were stored in our own maintenance supply area, which was nothing more than an empty truck trailer parked behind the plant. But that was about to change. A previously empty corner of the plant had been designated as our new parts storage area. Fortunately for me the maintenance manager recognized that I had good organizational and project management skills. So he put me in charge of the entire set up of the new parts area. Everything from designating specific storage areas by equipment type and setting up parts bins and labeling shelves, to inventorying our current spare parts, to physically moving the parts from the trailer in the parking lot to the appropriate area in the new storage system.

Being put in charge of this project, however, wasn't anywhere close to what I experienced anytime I was put in charge of something at my original employer. Here, all it meant was I was expected to do all of this by myself. But that was okay with me. It kept me busy all day long for several weeks, which kept me out of the sight of The Intimidator and his troopers.

Another bonus of this project was the fact that while I was working in the parts room I was exempted from the special assignments the rest of the maintenance department were subjected to like going up on the hot tin roof in the middle of the summer heat of southern Georgia to repair leaks and clean gutters, dig up old sewer lines and pump out septic tanks.

The entire shut down process lasted several months and was every bit as crazy as the original construction process. A few of the highlights of what I've affectionately coined "insanity take two" included another maintenance man being fired for wanting to go home after working a 12 hour shift (on the Fourth of July, no less), massive confusion, arguing and finger pointing between maintenance, management, engineering and equipment vendors over schedule delays and layout confusion and of course lots and lots of yelling, screaming and swearing.

Then there was the antics of the Spanish-speaking production workforce that could have almost been funny had their actions not been so blatantly dangerous. Among other things like painting some maintenance men's personal tool chests in the maintenance shop with primer and Rust-oleum (including my $250 roll around) they were also caught cleaning chains on processing equipment in the raw room with gasoline, filling the atmosphere with gasoline vapors while contractors were welding in the attic above them. But that was considered minor compared to the day they were sent up to the attic to clean up after the contractors and began by opening a door and heaving all the left over construction materials from the second story down to the ground in a free-fall—including a couple of full acetylene gas cylinders.

And of course maintenance was blamed for this craziness because we were told any maintenance employee had authority over all production workers and we were responsible for making sure they didn't do any damage to equipment or property or get hurt—in spite of the fact that we couldn't communicate with any of these production employees. Somehow we managed to survive and geared up for another start-up.

I thought I was prepared for what I knew would be complete pandemonium in The Intimidator's world of chaos. But in their usual fashion, upper management had yet another monkey wrench to throw in the gears of employee morale. Apparently, management felt The Intimidator was on the right track but couldn't quite get there on his own. If they could just find a way to ratchet up the misery index a little bit more. If they could just find a way to make the employees on the floor feel a little more threatened, intimidated and worthless. If only they could find someone a little bit meaner, nastier and more unreasonable than The Intimidator, then, perhaps, they would finally achieve the results they expected from this facility. Allow me to introduce you to a man I'll refer to as The Enforcer.

The Enforcer took over as reigning plant manager in the original facility. But he was sent to the cook plant on "special assignment" for the start-up of our hardly-used but new and improved facility.

The Intimidator was methodical in his meanness. Many times he would make his presence known in a room by simply standing there in an almost statuesque manner, allowing the menacing look on his face to speak for his dissatisfaction as he stared down each employee on the floor, one by one. He would eventually position himself close enough to make it unmistakably obvious he was watching a particular person with his menacing scowl. He would then motion a supervisor or manager over to where he was standing. Usually with his arms folded tightly, but occasionally pointing straight at the person he was previously staring down, he would lean in towards the supervisor he had summoned and make it obvious he was talking about a particular person, while deliberately keeping the volume of his voice just low enough so the person being discussed could not hear what was being said. On the occasion when he did speak directly to an hourly employee, it was always in a deliberate and unmistakably sarcastic tone meant to humiliate and never meant to motivate.

The Enforcer, on the other hand, was just an outright lunatic. He would come crashing through the door, screaming, swearing, feet stomping, arms flying—occasionally pushing and shoving things out of his way—literally ranting and raving like a rabid pit bull. He wasn't the first manager we had that employed this management style. But he was without a doubt the loudest. Not to mention the most irritating, arrogant and insulting.

Virtually all management in this facility prescribed to an "always the pilot and never the plane" philosophy. No matter what happened, it was always someone's fault. But The Enforcer took this philosophy to a whole other level. Nothing ever just broke in The Enforcer's mind. Somebody must have broken it. Likewise, moving parts never simply wore out no matter how many hours of usage they logged. Someone must have done something wrong to cause them to wear out. And even though they designed the entire facility as one long production line with one individual bagger (a design I tried to tell them they would regret from the first day I saw it) that had to shut down periodically throughout the day even if there were no mechanical failures for things like roll changes, coder ribbon refills and seal bar cleaning, the line was never—EVER—supposed to stop—not even for a minute. And when it did, of course, it had to be someone's fault. And someone had to be held accountable and pay for that fault. And The Enforcer was more than happy to make sure they did.

And just for the record, The Enforcer was not sent to replace The Intimidator. Oh, no, no, no. He was sent to "help" The Intimidator. So now we had two raving lunatics to contend with during this stressful start-up process.

Like Fred, I had countless instances where I felt insulted, mistreated and unappreciated. Usually a minimum of several times a day. But there is one seared into my memory more deeply than all the countless rest combined. One of the many things we needed but were not provided to properly do our jobs in maintenance was a laptop computer. We argued a laptop was necessary to properly troubleshoot the many PLCs (programmable logic controllers) that came in the majority of our electronic equipment. Management, on the other hand, argued that a laptop could not be trusted on the floor due to the high theft rate in the plant. So we were forced to troubleshoot the PLCs in this World Class, State of the Art facility manually with a voltage meter and schematics instead of simply letting a computer program do the troubleshooting the way these systems were designed to work.

But even more importantly, was the need of a laptop to program the date coder on the bagger. Date code formats vary greatly from company to company and from industry to industry. So they have to be programmed on site to fit the specifications for that particular product. The coder on our bagger came with one preprogrammed code date format and required any additional coding formats to be programmed on a laptop, utilizing software that came with the coder, and then be uploaded to the coder's memory. Once programmed in, the code format could be recalled and reused at will.

We used that default code format several times before chaos broke out on the floor one time when the quality manager announced in the middle of a production run the code format needed to be changed and we told her it wasn't possible without the use of a laptop. After watching the line sit idly for hours while mayhem ensued over this code issue, someone—I'm not even sure who, but someone—finally produced a laptop.

We quickly went to work programming and downloading the required code format, and in a matter of minutes we were back up and running. It's amazing how quickly unnecessary problems can be resolved simply by providing a workforce with the proper equipment.

Anyway, when the plant was redesigned that bagger was replaced with a brand new one. The one small problem was, management failed to order the optional date coder that was offered as an option with this bagger so we had no way to code our production. So, as usual, it became maintenance's responsibility to fix management's mess. I went out to the old warehouse where all the "useless junk" gets dumped and unburied the old bagger (that was approximately six months old). I removed the coder from that old bagger and managed to make it work on the new one. Crisis averted—at least for the time being.

Shortly after the second plant start-up utilizing the new bagger, we were told to prepare to run a new product the next day. This was another reason we had so much trouble getting this plant up and running properly once and for all. If it wasn't bad enough we had to deal with faulty equipment, out of control turnover, unsafe conditions, an incompetent management staff and a language disconnect between production and maintenance, we also had to deal with constant product changes. This entire plant was designed specifically to run one product; diced chicken. But like everything else, management just couldn't make up their minds what they wanted to produce. We switched from diced chicken to about a half dozen different types of frozen chicken breasts, to bone-in fried chicken, to sauced chicken wings. At one point in time, we were even bagging ribs in this so-called diced chicken plant.

One thing could be guaranteed with any of these new product ventures, there would always be mass confusion, chaos, last minute changes, borderline insanity, finger pointing, blame game playing and lots and lots of yelling, screaming and swearing. During my 22 years with my original employer, I saw more than my fair share of new product runs. And I saw them at one time or another from virtually every angle. There were times early on in my career where I was the mixer assigned to a new product formula and had research standing over me all day long. And there were times when I was an operator dealing with all the last minute surprises a new product can bring in the packaging aspect. And, of course, as a team leader I dealt with all of the above and more when it came to new products and new equipment. But the worst new product or equipment start-up I even experienced at that plant went a hundred times smoother than the best start-up here. That's why I always got an incredibly tight knot in my stomach anytime I heard the slightest whisper about a new product.

Remembering code issues from the past, coupled with the fact that upper management might not have even had a clue to the fact that we were still using the same coder that caused past issues, I decided not to play that crazy game again. We had four or five code formats programmed in the coder and available for use. I printed a sample bag with each of the available codes and did something I rarely did in this plant, I grabbed all the bags I had printed and headed straight up to the maintenance manager's office. I usually avoided the second floor at all costs. I saw much more of management than I cared to on a daily basis, usually while they were in my way and making it very difficult to perform my job in my work area. I was willing to make an exception to avoid yet another new product, three-ring circus.

So I marched into the maintenance manager's office with my sample codes and told him in no uncertain terms, "These are the ONLY code formats available for tomorrow's product run. Please get with the rest of management and find out what format they want set up for tomorrow." I went on to stress to him that if they wanted anything—ANYTHING— different from one of those exact formats, even if it meant changing one single character or switching two characters around, I would need either the laptop computer we originally had installed the coder software on, approximately five or six months earlier (and at least two or three maintenance managers ago), or any available laptop AND the original software disk that was given to the maintenance manager—whoever that was back then. And I told him if there were any changes to be made, I would need that laptop and software today so I could program and upload the code before leaving, to avoid any possible last minute confusion in the morning. There would be more than enough of that already.

I was given one bag back a little while later and told that was the code I needed to set up for the next day's product run. I reminded the maintenance manager again that this code could not be altered at the last minute and asked him if he had made that abundantly clear to the rest of the management staff. He said he had, and told me not to worry because the plant manager's entire staff had approved the code format he gave me to set up. So if there were any last minute changes, he assured me the blame would be squarely placed where it belonged, on upper management.

After the normal craziness that came hand in hand with all new product runs, we finally got the line started just before lunch. Shortly after bags of chicken finally started rolling down the conveyors, the quality manager came running into the room. With her arms swinging high over her head, and her face looking like that of a frightened deer starring into a car's headlights, she starts screaming frantically, "Shut down the line! Shut down the line!" I knew exactly what her next four words were going to be. And while I was waiting for those four stinging words to come blaring out of her mouth, I thought to myself, "Why do I even bother to try?" And just about the time I finished processing that horrible thought, here came the four words, "The code isn't right!"

So we went through the whole crazy laptop issue again. No one knew where the laptop we had originally used to program the coder had disappeared to. Someone produced another laptop, but it was worthless without the coder software. That software was stored with the laptop in the maintenance manager's office at one time. But that was at least two to three managers ago and who knows what was moved in and out in that time. Perhaps this plant's theft rate wasn't quite as high as everyone believed. Some of what they wrote off as stolen may have simply been misplaced by the revolving door of managers in this place.

So it was time for a plan B. There was a demonstration coder no one had any experience setting up or operating in the maintenance shop. It was left there by a salesman who had done a brief demonstration on it the day before. Two other maintenance guys dragged this thing down to the packaging area from the shop and the three of us dove in head first to try and get the line back up and running—with the proper code.

As soon as we attempted to fire this unfamiliar piece of equipment up, we got an error code. Not an error message in words that may have given us a clue as to what the problem was, an error code. A group of numbers that needed to be looked up in an operations manual to find out what the problem was. A manual we didn't have. We were to receive the operations manual, along with the full maintenance training session, if and when, the company purchased the coder. Until then, this unit was supposed to just be used as a demonstration model in the maintenance shop. We weren't even sure if this was a fully operational unit. But as usual, since we were maintenance technicians, we were expected to know all there was to know about this coder, as well as every other piece of equipment known to the world of manufacturing, rather we ever saw it before or not.

So while I struggled with the operation panel of this unfamiliar coder, frantically pushing buttons in a blind attempt to clear the error and my two counterparts stood on each side of me interjecting suggestions wherever they could, the air was suddenly filled with the unmistakable sound of The Enforcer entering the room, ranting and raving like a rabid pit bull all the way. "Great," one of my coworkers mumbled under his breath. "Just what we need, this loud mouth asshole in our way!"

There was a conveyor between us and the side of the room The Enforcer was on. He came storming up to the conveyor and went into his usual rant. Being the one with his hands on the controls, of course all the ranting was directed at me, the guy who did everything in his power to avert this whole scene of insanity over 24 hours earlier. And the most ironic part (if you consider pathetic to be ironic, that is) of me being the one taking the brunt of The Enforcer's temper tantrum was shortly before The Enforcer's entrance, the maintenance manager (yes, the same maintenance manager that had just assured me the day before that if there was an issue with the code format it would be management's fault and management's problem) had come in to see what was going on.

He literally stood right next to me while The Enforcer screamed at me like I was some kind of misbehaving child, insinuating I was everything from stupid and incompetent to lazy, worthless and lucky to even have a job. And my boss, the one who assured me I had nothing to worry about, didn't say one single word in my defense. I think he was just thrilled the ranting was directed at me and not him.

There's an old saying that goes something like "poor planning on your part doesn't constitute an automatic emergency on my part." But that was a saying this company wasn't familiar with. Management made asinine, half-thought through decisions all the time. Then expected maintenance to come in and bail them out. But if that wasn't bad enough in itself, they actually had the audacity to go around blaming anyone and everyone they could for their poor planning.

I've had my fair share of frustrating days, both here and everywhere else I've worked, over the last 30-something years. I've had days where I've felt overwhelmed, days where I've felt overworked and unappreciated, days where I've felt inadequate and days when I've felt just plain stupid. But never have I had a day on the job where I felt like I did on this day. On this day, I felt nothing but pure, unadulterated anger. As The Enforcer stood there yelling and screaming like a lunatic over a problem directly caused by management and frantically attempting to be corrected by maintenance—a problem that could have been avoided all together, no less, if someone would have just listened to the lowly little maintenance peon that tried to warn them of this possible catastrophe well over 24 hours in advance and now was somehow literally being verbally assaulted beyond anything even remotely close to what should be considered even moderately acceptable behavior on a workroom floor—I could feel every muscle in my body tighten up. I was literally cringing with anger. As my fingers continued to work the coder keyboard while my mind tried to block out the meaningless ranting of this overzealous moron, who in typical management style for this company was spouting plenty of criticism, along with tons of doom and gloom, threats and ultimatums while not offering anything even remotely close to a solution, my hands were actually trembling.

Then when he made the outlandish statement that he was going to call the manufacturer of the coder and ask them how long it was supposed to take to set this coder up, I had all I could do just to maintain my composure. "You better hope they tell me it's at least 30 minutes!" The Enforcer screamed out in his usual condescending and humiliating tone. "But my guess is they're going to tell me more like five minutes!"

Of course they were going to say five minutes. And that would probably be generous. It doesn't take anywhere close to five minutes to set up most coders under normal circumstances. Like when you are familiar with that particular make and model coder and you don't get an error code. Or you at least know what the error code means and how to correct it. Or if you, at the very least, have a manual to reference. But, of course, none of these scenarios applied to this particular situation.

At one point I removed my hands from the keypad and dropped them to my sides in frustration. Suddenly, I felt my hands starting to clench into fists. I literally wanted to punch this irritating moron right in his big, fat, loud mouth. For at least a fleeting moment, I actually think I understood what could drive employees to the brink of violence. My past management training included several sections on workplace violence. But never in my wildest dreams did I think I would be the one thinking about getting violent. It really took some serious mental restraint on my part to stop me from going straight over the conveyor and choking the living snot out of this bastard. Violence was not part of my normal personality profile. Words like soft-spoken, easy going and perhaps even timid were a much better fit. But on this day, I definitely wanted to hit someone.

But even more than hit someone, what I really wanted to do was quit. I wanted to walk out. Right there, right then, just like I had witnessed so many others before me do, many of whom had far more prestigious positions than me. But then I thought about my wife and daughter. I thought about keeping a roof over their heads, keeping food on the table and meeting my daughter's various educational needs. And to do that, I needed this job. Returning to Myrtle Beach wasn't even a viable option at this point due to the costs of relocation that this time would be coming out of my near empty pockets. Not to mention the fact that there really wasn't anything worth going back there for from a job perspective.

So I just stood there and took it. I took it like a defenseless little child that just got caught with his hand in the cookie jar. I stood there and allowed this man to scream at me in a far more humiliating and demeaning manner than any human being should have to endure. And over a problem his staff created and I attempted to avert the day before it could even happen, no less. As much as I wanted to throw all this information— along with a monkey wrench or possibly a hammer—in this bastard's face and tell him to kiss my ass on my way to the time clock, I just stood there and took it. I took it for my wife. I took for my daughter. I took for my landlord, the electric company, the grocery store and everyone else who had a claim to a share of my paycheck in support of my family.

But as much as I appeared to stand there and just take it, I didn't take it without a cost to the company. From that day forward, my steps in that place got just a little slower, my knowledge base just a little smaller, my sense of urgency not quite so urgent and my attitude towards my job in general went from dismal to done. From this day forward I would do what it took to keep my job, but not one iota more. Never again would I attempt to warn management of a pending problem. Never again would I find a way to make something work without the proper parts or equipment. Never again would I go above and beyond for anything that pertained to this company. And most importantly, never again would I put forth any genuine effort in any situation where a positive outcome would make The Enforcer look even slightly good. This was my official "Fred moment."

I did eventually leave that hell hole. Almost two years from the day I arrived. And like James—and Fred—I left on my terms. Of course my terms weren't as harsh as Fred's. As tempting as Fred's today notice sounded—not to mention that was probably all the company deserved—I opted to go with the standard two-week notice. Why? I really don't know. I guess that's just the way I am.

Of course, there was some vengeance in my resignation just knowing how badly the company wanted me to stay. I was actually called to the maintenance manager's office on my last day and offered an additional dollar per hour to stay. That wasn't something that happened very often at this company. And the sad part was by this time this was no longer the same company that I was so enraged with during The Intimidator and The Enforcer's reign of terror as well as all the not quite as bad but still mean as hell bastards before them.

It was still a pretty miserable place to work overall. But things had calmed down considerably. The Enforcer had been back home at the original facility for several months. The company had also hired a management consultant shortly after the second start-up who apparently made the company realize once and for all how damaging and dangerous The Intimidator's tyrannical management style was. That consultant eventually ended up being hired by the company as the new facility manager and he relegated The Intimidator to a desk job ordering supplies. That was perhaps the only truly happy day I can honestly say I spent in that facility.

We also had the most reasonable plant manager the cook plant had seen in that two year period by this time. Not only would he take the time to actually talk to me without screaming, swearing and threatening but he would also actually listen to me when I told him about specific problems we were encountering and occasionally even asked for my opinion.

That plant manager also brought in a new maintenance manager he worked with in a previous poultry facility. Out of all of our kinder, gentler, new and improved management staff, he was the one I cared for the least. He was the 12th, 13th—somewhere around there—person in charge of maintenance in the two years I worked there. And he came in with the same guns blazing attitude as so many before him that all failed

—threatening, intimidating, ready to show everyone who was in charge from day one.

But for the most part he did stay clear of me. I guess he realized I knew what I was doing and there were so many others in his department that did not. And he also had his hands full with a lot of young and immature maintenance employees that liked to wander and had issues with staying in their work areas for extended periods of time—especially in the refrigerated areas that were extremely uncomfortable. So we had sort of an unspoken agreement. I remained in the refrigerated packaging area where I belonged and did my job (while many times also doing the jobs of the production workforce and production supervisor making sure all the processing equipment continued to operate properly even when it wasn't broken) and he left me alone.

In many ways I was considered the packaging guru. I was the closest thing the facility had to an expert in the bagger and scales department. And that didn't happen accidentally. It was quite by design. I've always been somewhat of an opportunist. And I saw a huge opportunity to smother the reps from the bagger company and bleed them dry for all the information and training I could possibly suck out of them during the second shutdown. But I didn't do any of this for the company's sake. This thirst for new knowledge was motivated strictly by a desire to expand my personal knowledge base—not to mention my resume.

At this point I had had about all I could take and had both feet pointing straight at the door. I was just waiting for the right opportunity to come along.

And that was long before the inexcusable verbal assault I described earlier from The Enforcer over that ridiculous coder debacle. So my plan at that point was simple. I was going to become the best maintenance technician this company could ask for. I was going to learn the ins and outs of every single piece of equipment in my area of responsibility until I knew it all even better than the back of my own hand. Then I was going to take all that knowledge to a company that believed in treating employees with mutual respect versus trying to control them with threats and intimidation.

And even though this was now a kinder, gentler management, it was far too little and far, far too late for me. I was angry. And nothing was going to change that. The coder incident I elaborated on earlier was just one of dozens of similar fiascos. Like the time we were experiencing electrical problems with a spiral freezer. Josh opened the electrical panel door and discovered when sanitation covered the door panel with plastic to keep it from getting wet they tucked a large piece of plastic inside the lip of the panel door which stopped the door from closing properly and allowed water to seep into the panel through the misaligned door all night long while sanitation was doing their wash down, thus causing multiple electrical components inside the panel to short out.

But as usual maintenance got the full blame. Management, in all their brilliance, deciphered that because maintenance opened the electrical panel door, we were responsible for letting the water in. I guess the fact that there was already an existing problem which caused us to open the door in the first place was beyond rational thinking in their twisted logic. So while Josh and I were frantically troubleshooting the panel trying to determine which components were good and which ones were fried, in stormed Mr. Helpful—AKA, The Enforcer.

"Don't worry guys. I'm going to help ya'll," The Enforcer screamed in his usual sarcastic tone. "I'm going to help ya'll all right. I'm going to find out what maintenance man opened that door and I'm going to send his ass to the house! That's right. I'll show you how to handle this. Someone is getting their dumb ass sent to the house just as soon as I find out who opened that door!"

He stood just a matter of a few feet behind us, screaming phases like the ones above over, and over, and over again like a damn broken record. And he continued this verbal assault the entire time we were working in the panel. He had me so frazzled after several minutes of this nonstop tirade I was having difficulty touching the probes of my voltage meter to the proper wire terminals because my hands were actually trembling— and I wasn't even the one that opened the door!

Then there was the time that I spent over two hours first thing in the morning working on a problem in the spiral freezer that, if left as was could have resulted in the entire spiral conveyor belt jumping track. This would have resulted in the freezer—and ultimately the plant—being down for a minimum of two to three days. My thanks for all my efforts? The maintenance manager informed me the next day that he was going to have to write me up because the bagger was not set up in time. A responsibility normally associated with the production workforce, for the record, at every other plant I ever worked at or visited. And a responsibility that was supposed to shift to production in our facility in the event I was tied up with real maintenance issues on other equipment in the room. He also told me The Intimidator wanted me suspended, and possibly even fired for the incident, but convinced him to go easy on me because I did not have proper support from production. Well now, wasn't that generous of him.

And these are merely a couple examples of everyday business as usual in the maintenance department at this facility. If I were to document every incident similar to these examples just during that second start-up disaster in this facility the content would be so massive, it would be an entire book in itself.

I was also still extremely angry with the original management staff and their early and numerous predecessors over the way the original maintenance staff was bullied, abused and literally ran off. I got along well with all my countless maintenance counterparts that came and went over those two years, many of whom were younger than my old-est son. I even personally mentored a few that showed a real desire to learn the bagger and scales that most of the plant, for whatever reason, seemed to shy away from. I also developed some short-term friendships during this time and actually even learned a little something from many of those younger and less experienced maintenance guys that made their way through the cook plant.

But these weren't the guys I signed on to work with. In my initial interview, our original maintenance manager, as well as the personnel manager and the refrigeration manager who were both assisting in the interview process, discussed with me in great length the background and experience level of the members of the maintenance crew that had already been hired to this point. They also assured me these same guide-lines were going to be followed in filling the remainder of the open main-tenance positions for the cook plant. And they were true to their words. When that original crew was assembled in its entirety, there wasn't a maintenance manager on the planet that wouldn't have killed to have such an experienced, skilled and diverse crew. In many ways, I felt like the village idiot when I stood in the same circle with these maintenance connoisseurs.

These were the guys I moved hundreds of miles to work with. But in less than a year, they were all gone, including the three managers respon-sible for bringing us all together. And with the departure of those three managers also went the high standards set for the original maintenance crew, opening the door for a Myrtle Beach style "whoever is willing to work the cheapest is the most qualified" standard I thought I moved far away from.

The only exceptions to the mass exodus of that original crew were Josh and I. It was probably more coincidental than anything meaningful that the oldest and youngest from that original crew were the last two standing. But in any case, it was finally my time to move on. And with The Intimidator and The Enforcer still employed at this company in any capacity, I was jumping on that opportunity and getting out while the getting was good. After all, this company had trusted these two to rule as they saw fit once and with this company's reputation for impatience and quick changes there was no guarantee they wouldn't get impatient and resort back to these two at any time. And there was no way I was going to chance being subjected to that again. Not for an additional dollar per hour. As a matter of fact, I wouldn't have even considered it had they offered me an additional $10 per hour.

So I gladly handed the title of Sole Survivor of the original cook plant maintenance crew to Josh and went on my merry way to a very successful and rewarding (not to mention, at least in my humble opinion, well-deserved) career as a Field Service Representative with an incredible company. A job I have enjoyed now for six years and counting, with a company that treats their employees well, pays well and provides adequate benefits.

But as much as this sounds like the end of the story, it's really only the end of half of the story, the half that concentrates primarily on low wages and abusive management procedures. There was so much more I discovered during my two years in the poultry business about unsafe working conditions, inadequate facilities, illegal immigration and how all these factors tie into low wages that I realized all of these topics deserve at least a full chapter of their own to fully explain. So the next several chapters in this book will take an in-depth look at these topics beginning with how many companies utilizing illegal labor also skirt around many OSHA regulations and other safety standards.

Chapter 15. OSHA: Obvious Safety Hazards Accepted

Long before the first bags of chicken processed in this brand new, State of the Art, World Class facility had time to start collecting dust on the store shelves, I witnessed the facilities first serious accident. A young Mexican girl came cautiously walking down the steep, slippery platform stairs so many others had already fallen down. A pair of coworkers trailed behind her on each side, holding her by the shoulders to prevent her from meeting a similar fate. Her face winced with pain. Upon closer observation, I noticed the steel probe for a digital thermometer driven deep into the palm of her hand.

Due to the language barrier between production and maintenance, coupled with management's communication policy of "tell them next to nothing," I have no idea exactly what happened that day. Obviously this woman was trying to take an internal temperature reading of the chicken coming out of the freezer and somehow ended up poking the steel probe into her own hand.

It seems common sense would dictate that if you have a piece of chicken that is frozen solid and you attempt to force a sharp, steel probe into the center of the frozen meat, there will be a good chance that the probe will slide off the frozen, slippery surface. And given the amount of force required to attempt to penetrate frozen meat, common sense should also dictate that when that probe does slip off the frozen surface, whatever it does end up penetrating, it will penetrate deep and hard.

So am I suggesting this woman had no common sense? No. We all have lapses of good judgment at times that cause us to do things that rational thinking would rule against, especially when trying to hurry.

But yet another possible extenuating circumstance to this accident may have been the fact that this occurred somewhere around 8:00 in the evening and the majority of us had been running full-force since 6:00 in the morning with no relief in sight. We were all exhausted—both physically and mentally—after a very long day of trying to meet a full shift's worth of production in a facility that was quite frankly nowhere close to ready to run at full speed. And to add to the frustrations of the day, we had been subjected to the relentless hounding of an overly-aggressive, mean-spirited management staff that ruled through fear and intimidation and were rife with unrealistic expectations, yelling and screaming profanity-laced statements like, "move your ass," "you've got five minutes to get this line running or I'm sending all your dumb asses home," and "shut up with the lame excuses and make it happen."

Then there was the saga of the CO_2 freezer. A few of us in the maintenance department received about 15 minutes worth of training on this freezer from the installers. It was basically, here's where you turn it on, here's where you turn it off, here's how you increase or decrease the CO_2 level, etc. As I stated in chapter 1, this was far from the in-depth training that should be required before operating and servicing a piece of equipment where improper operation or malfunctions could be fatal. But we went into production flying by the seat of our pants with this freezer the same way we were winging it with just about everything in this operation.

As much as we tried, the exhaust system problem seemed unsolvable. We tried every possible combination of temperature, CO_2, and exhaust fan settings, but the problem just continued to reoccur. Occasionally, we would get a little insight from engineering, usually in the form of a new combination of exhaust fan settings to try. But for the most part, we were on our own.

Finally, one day as the CO_2 fog was about to reach everyone's eyeballs, and we raced around beating on exhaust pipes and opening doors trying to vent the room as people came in and out trying to minimize their exposure to the CO_2, one of the company owners saw the rising CO_2 fog through one of the upper level windows and ordered the line shut down and the room vacated. A few minutes later he walked into the change-out room we had all evacuated to. He immediately went into what appeared to be a very sincere apology. He stated that there was entirely too much CO_2 in the air in that room and again apologized for the fact that all of our safety had been jeopardized and assured us this would never happen again.

Unfortunately, this sincere concern was extremely short-lived. I don't know if the owner of the company was just giving the politically correct script while hiding behind his management staff and forcing them to do all his dirty work or if the management staff actually had the authority to override the owner's decision. But in either instance, within minutes of the owner's exit, the plant manager, along with a handful of his cronies, entered the room and ordered us all back into the packaging area to restart the line. And within an hour, the CO_2 cloud again began to slither across the floor. But no one seemed to care.

I can't remember how many more times that room had to be evacuated due to excessive CO_2 levels. And the most frightening part was the employees working in the room had to depend on their own senses to know when the CO_2 exposure level was getting too high and having an adverse effect on them. The room was equipped with a CO_2 monitor but amazingly, it never went off. There were numerous theories as to why. The most sensible one being the sensor was installed too high from the ground, meaning the CO_2 gas would affect the average height human before setting off the sensor. But in any case, there was never any more urgency placed on the CO_2 sensor than there was put on the CO_2 exhaust problem itself. Upper management had more important concerns like finding ways to make the line run faster and cutting down on waste and spillage. One day the plant manager noticed small pieces of diced chicken spilling out of the bottom of an incline conveyor. The line was shut down for repair immediately. Spilling chicken was worthy of shutting down the line for immediate repair. Potentially fatal CO_2 spilling into a room full of people with a defective monitor, on the other hand, was something that could wait until tomorrow.

That potentially deadly freezer eventually was removed, but only after one of the impromptu evacuations led to a security guard calling the fire department. He found a pregnant woman from the packaging area wandering around outside on the sidewalk screaming she couldn't breathe. He panicked and before anyone realized what was happening the fire trucks came rolling in. Once the local fire department started asking questions about the atmosphere in the affected area, the malfunctioning CO_2 monitor suddenly became a priority. Shortly after that, the packaging area was redesigned and the CO_2 freezer wasn't invited back.

The infamous CO_2 tunnel freezer was replaced by a spiral nitrogen freezer. The good part was that unlike the tunnel freezer that had CO_2 spraying throughout the tunnel (which had several possible escape points due to the freezer having large openings in the front and back of the tunnel, as well as six side doors that had seals that could potentially leak), the spiral freezer was far more contained and much less likely to ooze nitrogen into the atmosphere. The downside was that, unlike CO_2, which you could see and smell, and where the effects of exposure crept up slowly, nitrogen is invisible and odorless, and over exposure brings on an immediate lack of consciousness.

One thing that nitrogen freezer did have in common with the CO_2 freezer was the quality of training we received before being expected to operate and maintain it. This is where you turn it on, this is where you turn it off, this is where you increase or decrease the nitrogen level, etc., etc., etc... We began mentioning to the maintenance manager at that time we needed a full blown training session on operating this freezer before the installation team left because none of us were familiar with nitrogen based freezers. When mentioning didn't seem to get the point across we began hounding and eventually almost begging. But the badly needed training never materialized.

That is until the day an under trained and overzealous maintenance man opened the door and ran into the freezer without allowing the nitrogen to vacate from the enclosed area and fell flat on his back, immediately rendered unconscious from the oxygen depleting gas. Shortly after this incident, we were all sent to a training session explaining the dangers of working with nitrogen. We still didn't receive any training on the operation of this particular freezer, but something is better than nothing, I suppose.

Fortunately, an alert and quick thinking nearby co-worker fell to the ground and crawled into the freezer on his stomach to drag his unconscious coworker out of the freezer and to safety. Had it not been for the quick thinking of this man, our nitrogen safety training would have been the most tragic possible example of the old adage "closing the barn door after the horses are gone."

Examples of faulty infrastructure in this building were almost countless. I remember the first power failure the plant suffered shortly after beginning operations. We were in the middle of setting up equipment and the entire plant went dark. Luckily, I had a flashlight in my toolbox, which was almost within my arms reach. And this was the only light available to lead myself and several co-workers out of the pitch black room, full of trip hazards. There were emergency lights mounted all over the room. But, for whatever reason, not a single one came on.

As we were walking out Fred looked at me and said, "How the hell do you get an occupancy permit for a building without working emergency lights?"

And that was a good question. I remember the one and only fire drill conducted during my two year stint in this facility. All the maintenance men were called over the radio and instructed to tell everyone in our respective areas to evacuate because we were having a fire drill. That was a trick in itself considering most of the people we were trying to tell to get out couldn't understand what we were saying. So apparently, the fire alarm worked as well as the emergency lights and CO_2 alarm. So again Fred's question comes into play. No fire alarm, nonworking emergency lights, defective gas monitors, there was also an issue with the fire suppression system on a deep fryer from day one and there were consistent problems with the sewer system backing up.

How did a company with a brand new facility in this condition get a permit to occupy this building and begin production? Or, perhaps the question should be, did they get a permit? Were they even required to get a permit? This plant was located on the edge of a small town, in a small county in the middle of rural Georgia. Perhaps there were no permit requirements in this almost invisible to the rest of the world, little rural county. Or perhaps special exceptions were made for the company due to their vast land holdings and business interests in the area. Or, based on the way this company ignored OSHA regulations and laws pertaining to hiring illegal immigrants, perhaps they just ignored permit requirements as well.

As invisible as this place seemed to be to the outside world, however, there were government USDA inspectors on site at all times. So why these safety issues weren't brought to the attention of OSHA by the USDA is a mystery to me. I remember one time overhearing a couple of managers shortly after we started production saying the plant manager was tipped off that the USDA would be looking for OSHA violations as well. Really? If they were, all I can say is they must have been looking with their eyes closed because signs of unsafe conditions were clearly visible for anyone even casually looking in their spare time.

For starters, there was the issue of CO_2 fog slithering across the floor anytime we turned on the CO_2 freezer. Then there was the company's standard operating procedure of bypassing instead of replacing faulty safety switches.

My personal favorite was the safety switches on the high speed dicers. These safety switches were present on all doors and guards. They were designed to immediately shut down the dicers anytime one of the doors or guards were opened exposing the fast spinning and extremely sharp and dangerous blades. But since bypassing the safety switches was faster—not to mention cheaper—than replacing them, bypassing became the preferred fix—even though these actions presented an enormous safety risk.

The most egregious example of this was during the second start-up. A dicer was experiencing an intermittent power loss. The power loss was traced back to the safety loop that included all the safety switches but we couldn't pinpoint the problem to a specific switch. We struggled with this problem unsuccessfully throughout the remainder of the day and the problem was eventually turned over to a second shift electrician from the original plant. When I returned the next day I was informed that the dicer was fixed. I was also told not to mess with it anymore.

That was enough to get my curiosity up. So I strolled over to the dicer to sneak a peek at the so-called fix. The fix was one added wire, a wire that bypassed the entire safety circuit and rendered every safety switch on the entire dicer worthless. I brought this to the attention of the maintenance manager and made it abundantly clear to him that every single door and guard could be removed from that dicer and the blades would continue to spin. So I told him I was going to remove the wire and attempt to fix it properly. The maintenance manager then told me again not to mess with it and informed me that if that dicer was not ready to run that afternoon both he and I would be out of a job.

Luckily, this was one of the few times we actually had a bilingual supervisor in the packaging area that could bridge the language gap between production and maintenance. I explained to her in great detail how crucial it was that nobody opened any doors or guards on that dicer for any reason even if it wasn't running because if someone was to have their hands near the blades and the start button was hit the blades would start spinning. I then practically begged her to make sure all the Spanish speaking operators were aware of this danger.

But even more frightening was the fix that was applied to the second dicer when it started experiencing similar power drops. There were three separate motors in the dicer. There was a motor that turned the in-feed conveyor, one that drove the cutting blades and one that ran the take-away conveyor. Each motor had its own separate drive in the unit's electrical panel. I'm not sure who fixed it. Or who—if anyone—approved it. But someone decided the best way to assure this dicer kept running throughout production without intermittently shutting down was to run the motor drives in manual.

Or to put it in laymen terms, the start and stop buttons on the operator's panel were disabled and the dicer motors could only be started and stopped in the electrical panel by someone who knew something about how these drives operated. So had something or someone got caught in the dicer belts or blades the belts and blades would continue to run full speed—even if the stop button was pushed—until someone got to the dicer, opened the electric panel and hit the manual stop on each of the three drives. That was providing there was someone close by that knew how. And apparently everyone went along with this lunacy because no one had the courage to tell The Intimidator or The Enforcer the dicers had ongoing, unresolved safety issues and needed to be shut down. I still can't believe no one got a finger, a hand—or worse—cut off by those dicers.

The lack of proper protective thermal clothing for maintenance men required to enter the freezer at subzero temperatures should have also been another obvious giveaway that safety was ignored in this facility.

Sometime after our second start-up, well past a year after the plant originally went into production, someone finally ordered freezer suits and thermal gloves for maintenance men required to enter the freezer. Needless to say, we were thrilled to see that. And supervisors and managers from almost every segment of the plant got in line to grab the credit, all claiming they were the one we owed thanks to for pushing the freezer suit purchases through, when in actually, they all owed us an apology for sending us into freezers for over a year without the proper protective equipment.

There was also the issue of the sanitation department spraying the entire plant down from time to time with full strength parasitic acid. Those were some of my favorite mornings. Many days the overpowering stench of acid could be detected on the sidewalk before even entering the building. Once inside the processing areas on those days, there would be a sea of watering eyes, scratchy throats and uncontrollable coughing.

And waiting until the fumes cleared out before entering simply wasn't an option in a world ruled by The Enforcer and The Intimidator. Everyone was expected to charge right in the room and start setting up as soon as they arrived—rather it was safe to do so or not. In addition to the days we were expected to work in an acid saturated atmosphere, there were also the days when sanitation didn't finish on time and we were forced to start setting up while sanitation was still wildly spraying water in every direction from the ceiling to the floor. If there is one thing possibly more miserable than starting the day off choking on acid, it's working all day in a refrigerated room wearing wet shoes, socks and occasionally even clothes.

I remember one morning walking into the packaging area while water was spraying in every direction and noticed two people holding up what appeared to be an impromptu plastic tent in an attempt to provide cover for someone who was welding a broken conveyor leg. If only the maintenance manager could see this was my initial thought. But upon closer observation, I realized the maintenance manager was the one under the plastic operating an electric welder on a wet floor, with water spraying over his head, no-less.

But somehow the USDA apparently saw none of this. The USDA almost came to our rescue once—almost. We were only running one shift (supposedly) but the processing areas would not stop cooking chicken until a predetermined tonnage was met, even if it meant keeping the entire facility operating with the same personnel for 16 hours or more. I would always see a noticeable decrease in production and efficiency that was pretty much proportional with an increase in waste, spillage and unsafe work procedures after about 12 or 13 hours that just continued to multiply exponentially as the hours rolled by.

Perhaps this is why at my original employer we were not allowed to ever force anyone to work over 12 hours a day under any circumstances. Not only were we not allowed to but according to all of our management training, this would have been highly illegal. Maybe labor laws had changed in the five years or so that had passed since I had left that company. Or perhaps there was a difference in the labor laws pertaining to maximum hours worked per day in Illinois versus Georgia. Then again, there was always the possibility that this practice was illegal in Georgia as well and like OSHA regulations and hiring standards, the company just ignored the laws pertaining to maximum hours worked per day.

A temporary USDA inspector filling in for a vacationing regular inspector obviously made the same observations I had and informed the company on a day when they ran until about 11:00 at night with the same crew after starting up at 7:00 in the morning (with the majority of the crew starting somewhere between 5 and 6 am) that was the last time they could operate that long with a single shift and from that day forward he would shut down the facility at 7:00 pm regardless of how much chicken was thrown away.

I showed up for work the next day at 6:00 am elated. What a relief it was to know I was only going to have to work 13 hours and then could go home. When it got to be about 7:15 and chicken was still pouring into the packaging area, however, I tapped the production supervisor on the shoulder and asked him why we were still being buried in cooked chicken to be packaged 15 minutes after we were supposed to be shut down. The supervisor informed me that the company had gotten a letter from the regional USDA office stating they could run as long as was necessary to meet their production needs. I think we ended up working until about 10 or 11:00 o'clock again that night. No thank you. No good job. No apology for being made to work that long for who knows how many days in a row. The only words spoken were something like, "we start set-up at 6:00 am tomorrow—don't be late!"

But perhaps even more troubling than the letdown I felt in the USDA for failing to act on the countless safety issues in this plant was the failure of the Georgia Department of Health to adequately take action during a health crisis at the plant. After approximately six months of confinement in this nuthouse, I was told to go to medical one afternoon for a Tuberculosis test. I thought this was a bit odd at first. But then I remembered this was the same company that sent me for a drug test after spending a considerable amount of money to relocate me. So I assumed this was something that should have been required when I was first hired and, as usual, the company was trying to play catch up.

The following day, Fred walked through the door for the afternoon shift with a newspaper in his hand and fire in his eyes. "It's nice to know we work for a company that tells you so little you have to read the local newspaper to find out what's going on in the place you work,"

Fred said with a sneer as he tossed the paper down on a table. I glanced down at the paper and read a headline that went something like this "280 employees test positive for Tuberculosis at local poultry plant." The follow up story a couple of days later brought the total up to well over 300. That follow up article went on to say the owner of the company stated he would cooperate completely with state health officials.

As employees of that company, however, our information regarding the circumstances of this serious health threat began—and ended—with the information available in those two local newspaper articles. The company never talked to anyone directly to explain the potential dangers we were exposed to or even to attempt to reassure us there was no real concern. Not only were there no spoken communications, there were also no written responses sent to employees, no place for employees to inquire into the situation—not as much as a notice on the bulletin board.

Had this happened at my original employer, there would have been mass employee meetings held immediately. Notifications would have been sent out, managers and supervisors would have been walking the floor to answer questions and the bulletin boards would have been bursting with up-to-date information. But not only was this place not my original employer, it was about as far away as a company could possibly get. And they wondered why they had so much trouble finding legal Americans to work in this place?

Now the entire time I worked for this company management vigilantly denied hiring any illegal immigrants. But seeing how since my departure, I've read on more than one occasion about raids on the facility that netted hundreds of illegal immigrants, I'd say it's safe to assume they were lying. And if not outright lying, at least wrong, and perhaps fooled far too easily by false documents.

But again, if there were that many illegal immigrants in that company, and the Georgia Board of Health was in there conducting TB tests, shouldn't they have made that observation? And let's give them the benefit of doubt and assume they actually were the ones that reported the use of illegal immigrants in that facility after the TB epidemic. Then what took so long? This epidemic occurred more than a year before I left that facility and the first raid I read about occurred probably over a year after I had left.

Chapter 16. Time to Shatter the Myth

Before the illegal immigration debate blew into what it is today, I remember on more than one occasion reading articles in Myrtle Beach's daily newspaper that stated many Myrtle Beach employers prefer to hire Hispanics over Americans because the Hispanics tend to be more dedicated, more reliable and harder working. Wow! How did that one get by the politically correct police?

Had those stories stated that Myrtle Beach employers preferred to hire whites over blacks because the whites tended to be more dedicated, reliable, etc., etc ... I can only imagine the backlash. Protesters would have converged on the paper's door step by the hundreds—perhaps by the thousands. Boycotts would have been called for, resignations would have been demanded and screams for written apologies and retractions would have flown in from every direction imaginable. The paper quite possibly would have even been run out of business.

And the backlash would have been no less severe—perhaps even more so—had the articles stated employers in the area preferred to hire men over woman or heterosexuals over gays. Yet, they slandered the entire American population, insinuating that as a whole, Hispanics are harder working and more loyal to their employers than Americans are and no one as much as batted an eye.

I, for one, never bought this myth. I didn't buy it then because I knew "dedication" was a code word in the Myrtle Beach labor market for someone who was willing to work extremely hard and long—many times in extraordinarily difficult or uncomfortable and sometimes even dangerous environments—for extremely little. And I certainly don't buy it now after having worked side by side with literally hundreds of "superior to Americans in the eyes of the media" Hispanics on a daily basis.

It became obvious early on at the poultry facility that the maintenance department was going to be held responsible for virtually every aspect of the manufacturing process in this facility, including responsibilities normally associated with the production work force such as setting up and operating equipment. And the reason for this was simple; the majority of the 99% Hispanic production workforce was incapable of performing these fairly simple day-to-day factory floor duties. And not only were we held accountable for the day-to-day production activities, but we were also constantly badgered by management to take on their responsibilities for supervising the production workforce.

I remember one day in particular. A supervisor was peering down on the production floor through a window in the plant manager's office we laughingly referred to as the "Ivory Tower." Apparently the supervisor was not pleased with the pace he was witnessing on the production floor. So he began screaming at me over the radio. "Tell those slack Mexicans down there to move their asses," the overzealous supervisor hollered to me as if I were some type of straw boss on an 18th century southern plantation. "Yell at them," he continued. "Make them understand English!"

Many days I felt like a $13.00 per hour babysitter in addition to a set-up man, operator, mechanic, electrician and electronics technician.

It's not that the majority of these "undocumented workers"—if using the politically correct term—were not hard-working. It was quite the contrary; they were extremely hard-working—but not anymore so then most American workers. Or at least, not more so than the average American when the average American is properly motivated with sufficient wages and proper treatment. And for the most part, with the exception of sweeping the floors or pushing boxes around, most of these undocumented workers were clueless as to what to actually do. They had no experience and no skills. Quite a few were also extremely young and were probably seeing the inside of a factory for the first time. And again the language barrier came into play. Management wanted us to take these people under our wings and show them the ropes. But how were we supposed to do that when we couldn't explain anything to them?

I'll never forget the day one of the owners of the company approached me hollering about the metal detector. It seems he saw some production workers take bags of chicken out of a rejection bin by the metal detector (which means they could possibly be contaminated with metal) and returned them to the product conveyor after the metal detector, failing to run them through the metal detector a second time to confirm they were indeed false positives. He told me I needed to keep an eye on the production workers working near the metal detector to make sure that didn't happen again because he didn't think some of them understood what a metal detector actually was—or did.

Of course my response was, "okay." After all this was an owner. But, my initial thoughts were if I see them do this, how do I tell them not to do it when none of them speak English and I don't speak Spanish, and more importantly, shouldn't they understand what a metal detector is and does if they are going to work in a food processing facility?

The entire episode made me mad. As someone who had made a 25-year career out of working in American manufacturing, it made me mad to see what American manufacturing standards were being reduced to for the sake of cheap labor. As an American citizen, it made me mad to think about the fact that this stuff was eligible to proudly wear the "Made in America" label when it was in truth made largely by citizens of Mexico and other Central American countries, primarily under third-world manufacturing conditions.

But most importantly, as an American worker, it infuriated me to think these were the type of people so many American employers were attempting to hoist up on a pedestal, claiming their work ethics are so much more desirable than that of the average American worker when in truth these employers were merely willing to overlook these undocumented workers lack of education, lack of communication skills, lack of manufacturing experience and lack of professionalism for the sake of having cheap, easily exploited labor at their disposal.

Another episode that made me reflect on this concern was one morning when we came in and were told that sanitation was running way behind because several sanitation employees were sent home last night because they came to work intoxicated. How could this be, I thought? With the exception of the manager and a couple of supervisors, the sanitation department was exclusively, 100 percent Spanish-speaking Hispanics. You know, the ones so many American employers praise as being so much better than Americans. This made me start to think. I had worked with literally thousands of people in my 25-year career at this point. I had worked with every kind of American there was. I worked with men, woman, black, white, northern, southern, well-educated, high school drop-outs, young, middle-aged, senior citizens—every kind of American imaginable as well as English speaking, legal immigrants from all over Europe, Asia, the Caribbean and the Middle East.

So I took a step back and tried to honestly evaluate my new type of coworker, the hundreds of Spanish speaking, illegal Hispanics I was now working with. The majority were hard-working, well intended, productive workers that showed up every day on time and were willing to stay as long as necessary to get the job done, just like the majority of Americans. In that majority, there were those exemplary stand-outs willing to go far above and beyond the normal call of duty, just like the stand-outs that can be found in American workers. There were also some that, no matter how hard they seemed to try, just couldn't perform their job duties up to the same standards as the majority of their coworkers, just like some Americans. There was also a small percentage that seemed unmotivated—perhaps a bit lazy—that just did not seem to put forth their best effort on any given day, just like a small percentage of Americans. And then there were those in that dreaded minority that were completely uncommitted and totally irresponsible. They couldn't seem to ever make it to work on time, consistently took days off, seemed to put forth no genuine effort, even on their best day, ignored all company rules and regulations, and even occasionally reported to work under the influence of drugs or alcohol, just like the dreaded minority of American workers.

So what makes these equal at best, Hispanic workers so much more attractive to certain American employers than their American counterparts? Of course, there's the cheap labor aspect. But that's just the tip of the iceberg. For starters, they are incredibly easy to take advantage of. On the workroom floor, they're timid little sheep. They respond well to threats and intimidation and never yell back. They will do pretty much anything they are told without regard to reason or safety. They don't know the first thing about US labor laws, haven't a clue as to the existence of OSHA regulations and will work any amount of hours required including 16-hour shifts or longer. They hesitate to report injuries that could result in costly settlements for the company and would never consider reporting an employer for anything for fear of being identified as illegal themselves.

Occasionally, a local or two would slip into the almost exclusively Spanish speaking, Hispanic production workforce. But they would usually disappear immediately after being subjected to the company's downtime policy. Anytime the plant went down, the production workforce was required to clock out and sit in the break room without being paid until the plant came back up. Sometimes it would be for 15 to 20 minutes at a time, several times a day, often it was hours on end and there were times where it would end up being for the entire day.

Can you image devoting an entire eight hour day or longer to a company and receive no compensation for your time? Well, it happened on more than one occasion at this company. I even remember one time in particular where the entire production workforce sat in the break rooms (many of them actually stood or sat on the floor because there weren't enough chairs to accommodate the entire workforce) for the entire day on downtime on a Saturday no less.

This policy didn't apply to the maintenance department, of course. If the line was down for mechanical reasons, we were busy trying to get it back up. But even if the line was down for hours on end due to supply issues, we would continue to work doing preventative maintenance or something similar. This company may have treated us like dirt and had no real concern for employee morale or even safety, but I'm pretty sure they knew better than to try and pull something that outrageous on us. We were all Americans. And Americans are too smart to fall for this farce. If you are not paying for my time, then you do not own that time. And subsequently, you have no right to tell me where I have to spend that time. If I'm not being paid, I'm going home. End of story. Call me when you're ready to start paying me again and I'll come back. Perhaps the Hispanics would have adopted this attitude too if they weren't scared to death to complain due to their illegal status. But then again, if they actually complained about unfair treatment, they wouldn't have been viewed in such a favorable manner by this company.

CHAPTER 17. TWO-LANGUAGE SOCIETIES DON'T WORK

There was one thing I really didn't understand about this whole language thing. And it bothered me enough that if I spoke fluent Spanish, I think I would have had the nerve to ask someone. The million-dollar question I would like to ask is exactly this; how does anyone move to another country and expect to be able to get a job and function properly in the workforce without taking the time to learn the language spoken in that country? Again, I realize in the highly sensitive state of political correctness this country is in the midst of, this question seems out of bounds. But it needs to be asked. And even more importantly, it needs to be addressed.

If a person is not even willing to take the time to learn the language of the workroom floor, how loyal of an employee will they really be? Better yet, if they are not willing to learn the language of the country they want to live in, how loyal of a resident will they be? If they do not have enough respect for the people they want to work with and live with to make a concerted effort to be able to communicate with their coworkers and neighbors, how much respect will they show for their places of employment and neighborhoods?

I remember the personal language dilemma I experienced when we went for our training trip to Holland. Fortunately, English was spoken almost as frequently in Holland as the native language of Dutch, so we didn't have to deal with much of a language barrier. On our weekend off, however, we ventured into Germany where English wasn't nearly as pervasive. Between the four of us, we couldn't muster up two words in German and quite frankly, that made me extremely uncomfortable. We spent the majority of the day inside a rental car, driving around admiring the countryside. This limited our chances of making ourselves a nuisance to the locals due to our inability to communicate properly in the native language.

Of course, spending the entire day in the country required at least limited communication with the locals in the form of ordering lunch. With an almost endless choice of German restaurants we would prob-ably never have the opportunity to dine in again, we opted for lunch at McDonalds, a place we felt we could fumble our way through ordering without making fools out of ourselves.

As luck would have it, I somehow was the first of the four to make it to the order counter and test the waters for communicating an order with-out the benefit of being able to speak German. It was one of the strangest feelings I ever experienced. And it was all because I couldn't speak the language. I didn't even take the time to think about what I wanted. I was just concerned with walking up to the counter, finding a way to com-municate an order and walking away with any kind of food in my hand. And most importantly, I was concerned with doing all this with the least amount of confusion as possible. I ordered a number one combo meal. That wasn't really my first choice. But it seemed like the easiest order to communicate. I also always order my burgers with no onions. But again I felt I didn't have the right to special order due to my incompetence when it came to communicating in this country. So I pointed directly at the number one on the order board with one hand, held up one finger with the other and shyly mumbled something like "a number one please." I as-sumed I communicated my message properly because the cashier totaled my order. So I shut my mouth and didn't say another word.

As uncomfortable as that entire situation was for me, I can't even be-gin to imagine what it must be like to show up on a jobsite without being able to speak the proper language and expect to fit in. Yet people do this in this country by the millions on a daily basis. But dare to mention that this somehow does not seem feasible, or question the safety aspect of working around potentially dangerous equipment with people you can't communicate with and somehow you're branded a racist. It is something I will never understand.

The first plant I worked in never had a problem finding American born citizens to work for them. But there were a small percentage of im-migrants from right there in the neighborhood the company had hired, largely, I believe, to show support for the neighborhood they were part of. Not only did this plant strive to be a good employer, but it also strived to be a good neighbor as well. The plant was situated in a residential neighborhood that had a large Lithuanian population and many of them worked in the plant. There were also immigrants in the plant's workforce from many other European countries such as Poland, Hungary, Albania,

Germany and Russia as well. Their overall percentage in this workforce was small, but they were definitely there.

I found these immigrants fascinating. It was with great pride that most of them boasted about their rocky road to America. All the paperwork, the waits, the disappointments, the additional paperwork and more waiting, the wondering if it would be all they heard it was, the struggles to learn the language, then finally one day, the excitement of their long awaited journey to America.

Their accents were all unique. Some mastered the English language almost flawlessly, while others spoke in such a broken fashion they had to repeat many things twice. But, the one thing they all had in common was, they all spoke English. No matter how broken, no matter how badly, they all spoke English.

Many could ramble on for hours about the joys of living in America. With the exception of their thick European accents and tales of hard times in the old-country, they were ordinary, everyday Americans. They were proud Americans, dedicated employees and ordinary neighbors.

As I would drive everyday though the largely Lithuanian populated, city neighborhood the plant was situated in, I really couldn't tell the difference between there and the primarily American born suburban neighborhood I called home. The yards and homes were maintained in a neat and orderly fashion. Well maintained, late-model vehicles proudly lined the streets and there wasn't a foreign flag or signs in foreign languages anywhere in site. This neighborhood was full of American people, living the American dream.

I didn't realize it at the time, but what a contrast I would experience some 25-odd years later when I drove a few blocks down the main highway running past the poultry plant into the town many of the illegal immigrants called home. Mexican flags flew on many of the dilapidated buildings; Spanish was the language of choice for the limited signage in the area and disabled vehicles, broken down bicycles, assorted trash, overgrown grass and weeds and live chickens littered the yards.

But now that I've gotten that off my chest, back to the language barrier. There's something to be said for working with the same people every day. As I touched on in Chapter 2, there is a certain amount of bonding that takes place among coworkers, almost like an extended family when months turn to years. But when the people working next to you speak a different language, the opportunity for that bonding disappears. And the whole time I worked in this facility I felt just a little cheated because of that. I was seeing the same faces everyday but knew nothing about the person that went with the face. I had no idea if they were married, had children, what they liked, disliked, where they lived... some of them could have even been my neighbors and I would never know it unless I happened to see them out in their yards.

I've always been a people person and talking to coworkers during lulls in the action was always my favorite way to pass the time and help the day go by. But that wasn't an option here. Many times I was the only employee in the entire packaging area that spoke English. So in addition to being cold, being screamed at over the radio every time a piece of equipment went down, and basically hating my job and the company I worked for, I had to deal with the added misery of going sometimes days straight without having any meaningful conversation with another human being. I might as well have been working alone in a room with rubber walls. Many days I would have actually preferred that. Especially on the days when I was getting my rear-end chewed up and spit out because of mistakes being made by production workers, mistakes that I was expected to correct and couldn't because I couldn't explain to them what they were doing wrong.

The majority of the employees at this company seemed to have little, if any, desire to learn English. And quite frankly, that bothered me because I had no intention of learning Spanish. And to work together, we somehow needed to be able to communicate.

There were, of course, the exceptions to the rule, however, that actually tried to seize every opportunity possible to improve their English. They would come into the break room pointing at tables, chairs and vending machines and ask, "How you say this in English," or "What you call that?" And I was more than happy to help wherever I could. That's when I began to realize just how challenging English can be. I remember one day a young Mexican man who had a decent command of the English language walked into the break room while I was eating lunch. "Mr. Clyde," he said while pointing towards a garbage can. "What you call this?"

"Trash can," I responded without thinking too much about the question and the possibility of multiple answers.

"Trash?" he replied somewhat puzzled. "Not garbage can?"

I attempted to explain that garbage or trash can were the most popular names for the can but it could also be called other names like waste can or trash receptacle. Unfortunately, the more I attempted to explain, the more confused the young man became. I finally concluded the conversation by saying, "just keep calling it a garbage can and forget about all the other names."

Then there were the extreme minority I used to call language swappers. They would ask me what something was called in English. Then after I would tell them, they would tell me what it was called in Spanish. I must admit, I resented these "exchanges" at first, feeling as if these "foreigners" were trying to cram their language down my throat. And there was no way I was going to learn another language in order to communicate with people who refused to learn the language of the country they chose to move to.

But as time went on, I realized there was nothing scandalous about what they were trying to do. There was no hidden agenda to get the small handful of English only speaking people at the plant to secretively be coerced into learning Spanish without even realizing it. They were merely appreciative of the help they were getting with their English skills and attempting to offer something back in exchange for that help. So even though I had no desire to learn Spanish, I attempted to show enthusiasm and interest anytime I was given one of these impromptu Spanish lessons for the sake of not offending anyone. And I'm not referring to the politically correct definition of "offending" people. I could care less if I "offended" someone by making them feel like they were doing something wrong by speaking Spanish in America. As far as I was concerned, they were doing something wrong. We speak English in America, not Spanish. And I would guess I would not be very successful if I moved to Mexico and attempted to find a job somewhere where I could speak English. My only concern when it came to offending someone over this language disconnect was possibly discouraging someone from asking me to help them improve their English skills. And that was something I definitely did not want to do. If they were willing to put forth the effort to learn or improve their English, I wanted them to be assured I was more than willing to help.

But there were also some ironic, unexpected incidents in these impromptu English tutor sessions. I remember one hilarious event in particular. A young Mexican woman was attempting to push a lid back onto a Tupperware bowl after finishing her lunch. She apparently pushed unevenly on the back side and it launched the bowl, sliding it across the table and into a nearby chair.

"Oops," I said to the woman with a slight chuckle as she retrieved her wayward bowl from the chair.

"Oops?" she repeated back to me a little puzzled.

"Yes," I replied. "In English we refer to that as an oops."

A couple of days later, I was in the break room when the same woman walked in again. She glanced at me sitting at the table, reached into her bag, pulled out another covered bowl, hoisted it into the air, and hollered in my direction, "oops."

Apparently, without realizing it, I had managed to teach this young woman that oops in English meant bowl.

Chapter 18. Take Me to Your Cafeteria

A fellow team leader at my original place of employment once told me about her father, who was probably the toughest manager that facility had ever seen. He was giving a plant tour to some prospective employees and one young man asked about the cafeteria. The manager, short on patience and long on discipline, excused himself from the group and took the curious young man to get a glimpse of the cafeteria. That excursion was immediately followed by a personal escort out the door. She remembered her father telling her that if the cafeteria was all this young man could think to inquire about, he wasn't worth the company's time.

Hearing this story, initially I agreed. Of course that was also at a time when this was the only company I had ever worked for outside of high school jobs, and I assumed at that point that all places of employment provided adequate facilities for their employees. In light of some of the companies I have worked for since that time, however, I think it should be okay to ask to see the cafeteria. As a matter of fact, I think in the case of many companies now-a-days, it's a damn good idea to ask to see the cafeteria, as well as all the other employee accessible facilities.

The facilities a company provides for their employees say a lot about how much that company values (or does not value) its employees and their morale. Had I seen that "restroom facility" I described in chapter 1 the day I interviewed at the poultry plant, for example, that would have told me far more about that company than anything I could have picked up on during an interview with a manager.

And although that repulsive bathroom area was without a doubt the worst-case scenario of facilities, there were many other tell-tale signs of a lack of respect or concern for employees readily seen by anyone looking with open eyes. The cafeteria in the old facility was dull, dingy and dirty with hard plastic seats and grungy-looking drop ceilings. The back end of the cafeteria, an apparent add-on, didn't even have the dingy floor or grungy ceiling. The decor in that part of the room included cement floors, brick walls and ceiling rafters. Coincidentally, the maintenance manager left that outdated and dreary cafeteria off the plant tour the day I was there for my interview as well.

Unfortunately, as for the rest of the tour of the old facility, I put little validity on it because the maintenance manager kept reminding me I would be working in a brand new, state-of-the-art facility. And although the new facility, when completed, was the Taj Mahal in comparison to the old facility, it still left much to be desired from an employee comfort standpoint.

There was no cafeteria servicing the new facility. We were allowed to use the cafeteria in the old facility, but very few choose to. For starters, the walking distance from the new facility to the old one, combined with the slow service and long lines in the cafeteria, made it almost impossible to finish lunch and make it back to your work area in time. Not to mention the cafeteria staff were mostly rude and the food quality was sub-par to adequate on its best days and close to inedible on its worse. So the majority of us carried in our lunches and either ate in the small break rooms or went out to our cars.

The new plant was divided into three sections. Each section had its own break area and washroom. The break rooms were incredibly tiny and only had enough seating for about a quarter of the employees at once, even though the entire production force was supposed to punch out and sit in these break rooms every time the plant went down.

The small break rooms also doubled for locker rooms for the sanitation employees. I believe this habit was born more out of necessity than design. After all, the sanitation employees needed somewhere to change out of their rain gear. And since there was no designated place to do this, coupled with the fact that the lockers and the sanitation storage closet were in the back of the break room, there was an early morning take-over of these areas by the sanitation employees.

This was also the first room employees had to enter to clock in. The mornings when Sanitation finished on time and were utilizing the tiny room to get out of their rain gear and put away their equipment were the days I dreaded the most. The room would reek with the stench of human body odor almost bad enough to make your eyes water, as grown men—many of whom didn't have the greatest personal hygiene habits to start with—stripped out of soaked rain suits and exposed the clothing they were wearing underneath that was saturated with sweat from working in the hot, steamy, wet environment all night. Their smelly rain gear, some of which was still stained with wet, soggy chicken scraps and splashed with corrosive cleaning chemicals, would be strewn around the room, hanging on the backs of chairs or lying on the tables. The tables would also be loaded with dirty gloves, used mop handles, buckets and containers of cleaning chemicals waiting to be stored away in the tiny corner closet once the room cleared out and someone could actually find a path to put the stuff away. And these were the same chairs and tables the production work force would be expected to sit on and eat off of, in just a few hours when morning breaks started rolling around. This problem was eventually resolved when one of the original break areas was partitioned off and designated as the sanitation storage area. But, of course, this left one fewer break area and one fewer bathroom available for the rest of the plant employees.

The bathrooms were another matter in themselves. Two break areas had two single-toilet bathrooms each, one for men and one for women. The third break room had one single-toilet bathroom to be shared by men and women. Or to put it all in perspective, a grand total of five toilets (not five separate restroom facilities, just five toilets, and no urinals) for a manufacturing facility employing hundreds of people. And on top of that, the building contractor installed such poor door locks that if you simply pushed them in, they would pop out and unlock automatically when the door handle was turned from the inside. However, if you pushed in the lock and twisted it, it remained locked after you opened the door and stepped out; and once the door closed behind you, it could only be re-opened with a key. Well, these locks were way too highly technical for our workforce and the doors were constantly locked. Even after signs were posted on the door in Spanish explaining not to twist the lock button, the bathrooms were still constantly locked. This shouldn't have surprised anyone, however, since the small garbage cans in the washrooms were constantly overflowing with used toilet paper soiled with human excrement in spite of the fact there were signs posted in Spanish stating to flush used toilet paper down the toilet and not to throw it in the garbage can. So we had a grand total of five toilets for the entire workforce, with many—and at times all of them—locked and inaccessible. And once it was discovered that a bathroom was locked, it took anywhere from several minutes to a couple of hours to figure out who had a key and get them to come unlock the door, just for it to be locked again by the next person who used it.

Then one day, a fellow maintenance employee got tired of waiting for someone with authority in this building to correct the bathroom lock issue and went into self-help mode. He removed the guts from the lock on the men's bathroom door in the packaging area so the bathroom was accessible whenever he needed to use it. Problem solved—or at least that problem.

Of course, he created an entirely new problem at the same time. Since the women's bathroom was frequently locked, and the men's bathroom was suddenly never locked, we now had a situation where woman were occasionally walking in on men and men were occasionally walking in on women using the bathroom.

The most outrageous scenario happened to a young woman from the QC department one afternoon right before shift change. She told me that my boss promised to have the bathroom lock issue addressed immediately after she reported this to him. She was standing in the bathroom with her pants down, preparing to pull them back up, when a young man from second shift opened the bathroom door—with the entire second shift crew standing by, getting ready for their shift!

I don't know what the maintenance manager's definition of "immediately" was. But I do know that the young woman told me this embarrassing story shortly before I turned in my two-week notice and when I walked out the door of that hellish place for the last time, the infamous bathroom lock issues were still unresolved.

I also don't know why no one from management even seemed concerned with the bathroom door situation. But another thing I do know for sure is if we had inaccessible bathrooms and men and woman walking into the bathroom on one another due to faulty infrastructure in the facility at my original employer and no one from management addressed these issues, someone's head—and quite possibly multiple heads—would have rolled. But then again, that company never had to resort to hiring uneducated people from Third-world nations, most of who were in the country illegally, to fill virtually all of their entry level positions either.

So the bottom line to all this is exactly this; Illegal immigrants do not take jobs Americans don't want. Illegal immigrants make jobs Americans don't want. And they do this in many ways. They do it primarily by undercutting the wage base the average American worker expects in the same manner that the retired population create jobs in Myrtle Beach non-retired employees can't afford to take by undercutting the wage base the average family man can accept and still be able to support his family.

But as I stated back in chapter 15, illegal immigrants also create jobs Americans don't want by being willing to accept working conditions Americans won't—not to mention shouldn't. A prime example of this outside of the manufacturing industry would be recent comments I heard on the news made by a labor union leader in California concerning farm field workers. The union official announced he would be willing to offer jobs in the fields currently being performed by immigrants to

Americans but didn't expect any takers because it's extremely hot in the fields and many times there isn't any shade available.

Hello! Calling OSHA. Are you listening to this? Extreme heat coupled with no shade, and my guess would be also extremely long shifts with few, if any, breaks. Sounds like a recipe for heat stroke to me. Now I've never been a fan of massive, over-reaching government regulations that hinder business. But by the same token, some oversight is necessary if unscrupulous employers are taking unfair advantage of employees and possibly even putting them in harm's way. That's why both labor unions and government bodies like OSHA and the Department of Labor were originally established.

And it seems to me like this extreme heat and no shade dilemma would be easy enough to resolve. How about something as simple as requiring these large farms in California (or any other hot environments, for that fact) to provide some type of shade along with regular breaks so the overheated employees can cool down. Something as simple as a screen tent, maybe even just a tarp supported by poles to provide some shade. Put a couple of cheap picnic tables under there with some large water jugs and a big stack of paper cups, maybe a couple of box fans powered by extension cords or a small, portable gas-powered generator and—Bingo—instant, affordable cool-down area.

Would this really be too much to expect from an American employer to make their jobs more attractive, not to mention safer, for American workers? And if the unions truly represent the best interests of their members, shouldn't they already be demanding this? Perhaps I'm not the best person to comment on unions, however, since I have never belonged to a union. I did work in a union shop once, though. The poultry plant, believe it or not, was actually a union shop.

I don't know what the actual union affiliation was at that plant but I do know they had one because when I was filling out my initial paperwork there were some union forms included in the packet. I brought the union forms to the personnel woman, explained I had never worked in a union shop before and asked her if I could get some additional information on the union before deciding to join if union membership wasn't mandatory at the plant. The woman didn't speak and simply reached her hand out in my direction. I assumed she was nonverbally asking for the papers so I put them in her outreached hand. Her arm rotated until the papers were positioned over the top of the trash can next to her desk where she quickly deposited the papers saying something like "you don't need to be concerned with that."

So perhaps this union was only for what would have been considered the non-skilled workforce segment of the plant. Or perhaps the company didn't want people that might actually expect the union to actually represent them against the company joining the union. Like I said, I really don't know much about union membership so this is all purely speculation on my part. I would see an occasional union notice posted on the company bulletin board from time to time but never paid them much attention because I figured they didn't concern me. But in any case, I do know one thing, if a union was actually representing the best interests of the non-skilled workers at this plant; I would hate to see how they would have been treated without anyone looking out for them.

SECTION IV. IS THERE ANY HOPE

Chapter 19. Where Do We Go From Here?

I've struggled for some time to produce an appropriate ending for this book. My original intent was to stop at Take me to Your Cafeteria. I thought that a compare and contrast of facilities at a good company versus not so good companies would be a perfect way to drive the point home. But once I was finished, it seemed to fall flat. So I thought about it some more... and thought about it... and thought about it. But nothing was coming to mind.

Then one Saturday morning I was lying in bed, trying to motivate myself to get up, while watching a rerun of Saved by the Bell (I don't know how many 50-something year-old, grown men would actually admit to that, but that is what I was doing). The show was about graduation. As I laid there and listened to the made-up farewell speeches and Valedictorian rhetoric, I started reflecting back on my own high school graduation. I don't remember any of the words spoken that day. I'm sure it was all the standard, "As we embark on our next journey" and "We are the future leaders..." But none of that struck a chord with me. I was thinking more along the lines of just give me my diploma so I can get out of here and get a job. I wasn't looking to change the world, just survive in it.

Then I started thinking about my youngest daughter's graduation which was a little over two years away. And as I laid there longer and longer, drifting deeper and deeper into thought, I started wondering what I would say to a graduating class in this day and age if I were given the opportunity. And the more I thought about it, the more I realized what I would say today would be far different from what I would have said 20, maybe even 10, years ago.

Years ago, I would have surely included something about finding a good, stable company you could develop a long term relationship with. I don't know if that is even a realistic option nowadays. I would have also most likely pitched manufacturing as a viable career consideration for those considering furthering their educations at a tech school or possibly passing on any further education at all like I originally did. But I'm sure I would skip that option today. If I did give any advice as far as preparing for a career in American manufacturing, however, it would definitely include something about majoring in Spanish as that seems to be the up and coming language of choice on American factory floors.

Fortunately, my daughter has nothing in common with me when it comes to high school as well as dreams for the future. She is in all honors classes for her core subjects. Her electives include two years of French. She has already selected her two top college choices and has also already decided on a major and a minor. And all this just seemed to happen with minimal encouragement from mom and dad. Oh sure, we encouraged every chance we got but there was also plenty of self motivation. I have little concern for her future.

But, what about up and coming graduates who have more in common with me than my daughter? I came from a long line of hard-working, blue collar factory workers, truck drivers and construction laborers. Sure, we had our small handful of misfits, just like in any other family—a couple of school teachers, an office worker or two, an accountant—but for the most part our office attire was far more flannel shirts and blue jeans than shirts and ties. And the dirt and grease under our fingernails, along with the bruises, calluses and scars on our hands, told the tale of how we earned a living.

We drank beer and occasionally whiskey, but never champagne or wine. We preferred backyard barbeques over five-star restaurants and campgrounds over fancy hotels. We loved steak and pork chops but often settled for hamburgers, hot dogs or meatloaf. None of us could give directions to the local opera house or knew what a symphony orchestra sounded like live, but we all were familiar with the sights and sounds of Soldier Field, Commisky Park, Wrigley Field, The Chicago Stadium and the local Saturday night stock car track.

We woke up early every morning, usually before the sun even came up, and worked hard every day. We braved inclement weather, morning rush hours, accidents, road construction and anything else the cold and sometimes crazy city of Chicago threw at us in the way of obstacles and always punched the clock on time. For the most part, we adopted the theme of the good-old, all-American mailman; neither rain, nor sleet, nor snow (nor hangovers from the beer and whiskey, for that fact) could keep us from reaching our destinations on time and performing our jobs to the best of our abilities. We went home at night feeling a well-deserved sense of accomplishment and pride. We earned every penny we spent on the above aforementioned pleasures and wore our determined work ethics proudly on our blue collar sleeves.

But where do people like this go now? Certainly not the original plant I enjoyed working at for so many years. They managed to chug along with their cost cutting for approximately five years after my exit before the always looming possible closure finally became a reality. Unfortunately, I almost completely lost contact with all my old comrades from that plant over the years and had little knowledge of what was happening at the time. But not too long ago, thanks to the advent of Facebook, I reconnected with a few of my former coworkers. From what I picked up through limited correspondence and reading status posts it sounds like the majority—if not all of—the products produced at that plant were sent to Mexico.

The cable manufacturer I worked for in Myrtle Beach wouldn't be an option for aspiring manufacturing hopefuls either. They closed up shop shortly after I was let go. I don't know any of the particulars of why the plant was closed, but I do know the quality manager told me long before my untimely dismissal that we were losing a lot of our contract work to plants with cheaper labor in Mexico. I find it quite ironic that the majority—if not all—of the products manufactured in the first two plants I worked in were sent to Mexico while the vast majority of the jobs in the third plant I worked for in America were given to people from Mexico. How's that for a double-edged sword?

Now, the poultry plant I worked at, on the other hand, is still a viable option for a career in manufacturing because the last I heard they were still in business. And they are willing to hire Americans for entry level positions. That is, providing the Americans are willing to work under the same conditions and for the same deflated wages as people from Mexico and other third-world nations. Again, the irony is almost sickening. The two plants that at least tried to play by the rules have long since been put out of business while the one that breaks, or at least bends, the majority of the rules rolls merrily on.

And there were also career opportunities available there for above entry level. I saw first-hand how easy it was for young 20-somethings, and sometimes even 18 year-olds straight out of high school, to land a career there in maintenance. Josh came to us about as prepared for a maintenance career as a kid straight out of high school could be. But he was the exception in this place, not the rule.

Many were hired because they had experience installing car stereos, working on farm equipment, or sometimes something as simple as working as a laborer for an electrical contractor pulling wire through conduit. Not that there was anything wrong with these types of backgrounds. Any of this experience would make a person a viable candidate for a maintenance trainee, but not a full-fledged maintenance technician—especially one required to work in 480-volt electrical panels. But there were no such things as training programs at this facility. You were hired, and you went to work, fully qualified or not.

My training started with the trip to Holland to train with our equipment supplier and ended with our two-week, state sponsored PLC training at a local tech college. The Holland training, although I must admit I loved, didn't amount to much help on the production floor. For starters, this appeared to be something included as part of the purchase package due to the large amount of equipment being purchased and was obviously funded primarily, if not completely, by the equipment manufacturer. And I believe the company used this supplier provided training junket to sway Fred, Keith and I, the three candidates the personnel manager later confessed to me were seen as instrumental to a successful start-up based on our collective experience, into a quick final decision. Now, I don't see anything wrong with this tactic, just for the record. Quite to the contrary, I think it made good business sense. They saw three people they felt could be instrumental to their organization and did whatever it took to bring those candidates into their stable. It's just a shame that after all the effort they put into making us happy; they failed to put any effort whatsoever into keeping us happy.

The training itself could be described as lackluster at best. It was primarily operator based training for the most part with a little sprinkle of maintenance training dusted on top. The only part I remember as being beneficial from a maintenance standpoint was when they explained the difference between the standard layout and design of European electrical prints and schematics versus American prints.

And the majority of the training for Fred and I would never be used because the majority of the equipment manufactured by this supplier was processing equipment for the raw and cook areas and based on our previous experience with packaging equipment, we were both assigned to the packaging area.

The PLC training, on the other hand, was entirely maintenance based and extremely beneficial. Or at least it could have, and should have been. But seeing how almost everything we learned when it came to troubleshooting PLCs was done through interfacing the PLC with a laptop computer and we did not have access to a laptop at the plant, most of the skills we learned were never put to use.

But as meaningless as my limited training seemed to be in the big picture of things, it was massive in scope compared to what new hires, after the original maintenance crew, received which, with the exception of the emergency nitrogen safety training, was pretty much nonexistent.

And when a company doesn't provide any training, it's difficult for their workforce to grow in their value to that company. As I've mentioned before, I found creative ways to provide my own training in that facility. The most beneficial for me was picking the brains of electrical whiz kids like Fred, Keith, James and Mike everyday and learning everything I could from them. Once they were all gone, however, that opportunity was lost forever because never again did the company hire maintenance employees of their caliber. (At least not in the two years I was there). I also took advantage of working closely with equipment installers and field service technicians, whenever new equipment was brought in, and I read every single equipment manual I could get my hands on. But none of this "training" as I refer to it as was done at company direction. It was all done on my own, and as I soon realized as replacement maintenance people were hired to replace the original maintenance crew, not all new hires were as resourceful as me—or at least not for $10 per hour.

My career, as most, could be compared to climbing a ladder. It needed to be taken one step at a time. And, of course, that first step, the one that actually put me on the ladder, was the most crucial. Had there been no line at that first plant I worked in for me to stack cases onto a pallet, I don't know where I would be today.

I originally stated that the whole episode started for me with a recommendation from a family friend. Actually, that is only partially true. I did receive a recommendation from a very wonderful lady who became a dear family friend, but she wasn't at that time. Truth be told, I met her a few days before she gave me the recommendation. My father had suffered from emphysema for 10 years. He became gravely ill and ended up sharing a hospital room with this woman's husband.

I was going to visit my dad daily and this couple started taking a liking to me. We would chit-chat regularly and it wasn't long before my employment dilemma came up. I had graduated high school in June. It was now October and I was still working as a cook at a steak house where I had worked part-time while attending high school. I was pulling down as many hours a week as possible while waiting for something better to come along. The couple was immediately eager to help, not only because they had taken a liking to me, but also my parents as well.

The gentleman (who became my father's roommate after an unfortunate fall from a ladder) was the first to throw out a suggestion. He mentioned that their son was a district manager with a large grocery store chain and he was all but sure his son could get me an entry level job as a grocery bagger at a store of my choice. That was actually not a bad job, back in those days. Most larger grocery chains back then started out their baggers for about the same hourly wage offered by most factories. And grocery baggers were usually promoted to stock boys (that's what they called them back then) rather quickly, adding a few more dollars per hour to their salaries. I thanked him for his offer and told him although I was primarily seeking a factory position, I would be willing to consider anything that paid more than the whooping $3 and some odd cents per hour I was currently making, especially if the offer included benefits, which the chain grocers did back then.

Then the gentleman's wife joined the conversation. She mentioned that the plant she had just retired from had opened a new department and was currently hiring. She went on to explain that it was very difficult to get hired there and almost always required a recommendation from a current or retired employee at the plant. Then she told me she would allow me to use her as a personal reference. She gave me the name of a woman in personnel to ask for, and told me to say I was an old family friend.

This little arrangement wasn't unconditional, however. The helpful woman explained she was doing this primarily because she knew my family needed help due to my father's deteriorating health. She also told me that in the short time she had known me, based primarily on the way she saw me at the age of 18 trying so hard to take care of my father, that she was confident I would do the right thing if I landed a good job and do all I could to help my family. She also told me I was only the third person she had recommended in over 30 years, the other two being her nephews. She was extremely proud of the fact that the only two people she ever recommended were both model employees. And she made it abundantly clear that if I did anything to tarnish her reputation, she would never forgive me.

Her oldest nephew was already a lead man in maintenance and eventually became a supervisor with over 30 years at that plant. Her younger nephew put in over 20 years there and also became a supervisor before eventually moving on to a position at corporate. And, of course, I followed them with 22 years of faithful service, the last six as a team leader. So, I'd say it was safe to assume her reputation was well guarded.

I was offered an opportunity to start almost immediately. I jumped on that offer immediately, without giving it much thought. I was happy as could be. The manager of the restaurant where I was flipping steaks while waiting for something better to come along, on the other hand, who made a work schedule two weeks in advance, didn't share in my euphoria. I had an outstanding relationship with the manager at that steak house. I respected him as an authority figure and he respected me as an employee and appreciated the job I did. But it went further than that. I genuinely liked him as a person and I believe he felt the same way about me.

So I walked into his office to announce I was leaving for a much better job, expecting a big smile, a heartfelt congratulation, a firm handshake and maybe even a big bear hug. What I received, however, was an icy glare, followed by an impromptu lecture about the evils of quitting a job without proper notice, something in all my excitement and jubilance I, quite frankly, never gave any thought to.

"I'm extremely disappointed in you," the usually friendly but occasionally stern manager said to me in a haunting voice that sent shivers up my spine. "Not only as an employee, but as a person as well," he continued. "I thought you were better than that."

"This guy can't be serious," I distinctly remember thinking. This was a job for high school kids, which I no longer was. He had to realize I was looking for something else since graduation. And after months of relentless searching I finally found something not only that I could hopefully count on far into the future but also at a time of great need for my family as well. He knew what was happening with my father. And now that I was finally seeing a slight ray of sunshine through all those clouds, he had the nerve to rain on my parade? And not just rain on my parade, but actually go as far as to suggest I should tell a company that was willing to pay me $5.00 per hour that I had to wait two weeks before I could start so I could continue to work a little longer for $3.00 per hour. Did this man not realize just how important that additional $2.00 per hour—not to mention a guarantee of 40 hours a week and possibly even overtime— was to my family right now with my dad in the hospital racking up medical bills? Just who did this guy think he was?

But after getting over my initial anger due to his less than congratulatory response to my good news, I tried to see it from his point of view. Most of the employees here may have been high school kids, but he wasn't. He was a grown man with a family to support and a business to run. And I was one of his strongest cooks. Not to mention he was gracious enough to expand my hours as much as he could on my request after I graduated, making my schedule of 30 plus hours per week far more difficult to backfill at the last minute than the average high school kid working a maximum of 15 to 20 hours a week. Didn't I owe him anything in return for that? This was perhaps my first real life experience as to my extended obligation to an employer beyond the obvious daily ritual of showing up every day and working hard.

So after we both cooled down a little, we sat down and looked at my schedule for the next two weeks. I cooked a lot of lunch shifts. And those were definitely out because of my new day job. But I also worked a few evening shifts, as well as weekends. So I agreed to work any evening and weekend shifts I was on the remaining schedule for, as well as any additional evening shifts I could pick up for anyone willing to swap with me and take any of the lunch shifts I had to dump, and he thanked me for my cooperation.

I remember my first week at that plant like it was yesterday. My first day was Monday, October 11, 1976. And my father passed away the following Friday, October 15. It was a week of highs and lows to say the least. Not to mention also a week of sheer exhaustion.

Some days I would go straight to the steak house from work, cook for a few hours, then head to the hospital until visiting hours were over. Other days I would go straight to the hospital for a quick visit then work the closing shift cooking steaks. Thursday I was originally scheduled to cook the early dinner shift. Then I agreed to take the closing shift as well so the person scheduled for that shift could pick up the Friday lunch shift that I was originally scheduled to work which meant no hospital visit for me that day. Even though I know that was the right thing to do from an employee loyalty stand point, it was a decision I regret to this day.

When I got home that night the first thing my mom told me was how great my dad looked and felt that night. She said he sounded strong, was in good spirits, and even sat up on the edge of the bed, something he hadn't been able to do in days. I couldn't wait to finish my day shift at the factory, then my dinner shift at the steak house on Friday so I could get to the hospital and see all this for myself. Unfortunately, my dad took another turn for the worse late Thursday night. By the time I got to the hospital Friday night he was tired, weak, and didn't even seem to be much in the mood for company. I apologized for not being able to come the night before and explained why. He seemed to understand. Then I made some small talk about how my first week on the new job went, told him I had one more week of pulling double duty on two jobs before things got back to normal for me, and went home when they announced visiting hours were over. About two hours later, we received a call from the hospital telling us to get back there ASAP, and by the time we arrived he was already gone.

I played this whole scenario back in my head the day I was let go in such a cold-hearted manner at the cable manufacturer, and it only served to anger me even further. I was willing to go to these lengths to show loyalty to a company I was leaving when I was working part time during high school, but a company I worked for full time (not to mention did one hell of a job for), one that was well aware of the fact that I had five children to support felt they owed me no more than 15 minutes. I understand things change in business and sometimes companies are forced to make cutbacks they would prefer not to. And that's basically what I was told by the quality manager. It wasn't his decision, and if it was up to him, he'd keep me. And maybe that was the whole truth and nothing but the truth, as they say. Maybe he didn't even know, himself, until shortly before calling back to my office. But somebody in this company knew this was going to happen well before those final minutes of that final day of the week. These aren't the types of decisions that are made at 3:00 o'clock on a Friday afternoon. The day before was payday. Had I known this then, I could have at least possibly made some adjustments in the way I allocated that second from last paycheck to ease the situation slightly. But apparently, after three years of faithful service, the company didn't feel they owed me even that much.

Even in the hardest of financial times for a business, there is still a right way and a wrong way to do things. And this was by far the absolute wrong way. The thing I found perhaps the most insulting of all in this whole situation, however, was the fact that the quality manager mentioned on more than one occasion that none of us should entirely give up hope because there was always the chance we might get called back if business picked back up.

Did he really think I would have ever even considered working for this company again after this farce? If I had been laid off in a dignified manner, with proper notice, I would have jumped at the opportunity to come back. After all, this plant had now become home to me. The quality manager was a few years at best away from retirement. It was already a foregone conclusion that our supervisor would be moving up into that role. It was also made known to me on more than one occasion that I was a solid front running candidate to move into that supervisor position when that time came. And even though this company was nowhere near as great to work for as that first plant I spent 22 years in, I felt as though I had a future there and had come to terms with the fact that this plant might be as good as it gets for me from this point on.

But within minutes of walking into that meeting room, I knew I was done for good with this company, no matter what. Deep cutbacks are sometimes necessary regardless of how valuable you may be to a company. But under these circumstances, there could have been snowball fights happening in hell, while pigs were flying and cows were jumping over the moon and I still would have never considered returning to that company. Trust is a fragile thing. And once it's been damaged, it's usually destroyed for life. Fool me once, shame on you. Fool me twice, shame on me. And my momma didn't raise no fool.

But anyway, back to my first week on my first full time job. As if I didn't have enough emotional turmoil churning inside me already, I also had the additional weight of worrying about possibly losing my job for taking time off on only my second week on the job. I didn't really think it would be a problem under the circumstances. But in the same token, I had no way of knowing that for sure. So I bypassed my supervisor completely and called straight to the personnel department first thing Monday morning to explain the situation. Not only did they assure me I had nothing to worry about but also told me under the circumstances they would allow me to take up to three days off with pay for an immediate family funeral leave in spite of the fact that I was a new employee and technically was not eligible for any company benefits until my probationary period was up.

So that was how I hopped on the ladder. Maybe not the most conventional way to begin a career, but regardless, from there I started my climb. And just like I did at the poultry plant some 20-something years later, I talked to everyone I thought could teach me anything about this new business I was now part of and took advantage of every training opportunity available. The only difference here versus the poultry plant was that most of the training opportunities I benefited from were company-sponsored as opposed to self-created.

From time to time I would run into a naysayer in my little social network of blue collar factory workers—usually someone who worked for a much smaller manufacturer—who would scoff at the amount of money I made for the job I did. And I must admit there were times, especially in the early part of my career when I was doing basic utility jobs that required very minimal skills or training, that I did feel like I was probably overpaid. But instead of letting people who worked for companies that paid less (and occasionally I would run into someone that worked for a company that paid a lot less) make me feel guilty, I would instead use those feelings of perhaps being a little overpaid as motivation to appreciate my employer that much more and use that motivation to remain a faithful employee even on what might be considered less than perfect days.

I remember one small party in particular that was thrown by a friend of mine. He worked for a fairly prominent regional plastics manufacturer known for paying far under the local average and hiring a lot of Hispanics with questionable immigration status. Yes, this was a problem as far back as the late 1970s. It just wasn't as widespread and flaunted—not to mention defended—as it is today.

I had recently won a bid to become a machine cleaner in the sanitation department. It wasn't a hard job bid to win. Not too many people wanted to work in sanitation. The majority of the department was made up of immigrants (the legal kind that spoke English, for the record). Machine cleaning was an extremely dirty job that also often included getting wet. And it was done exclusively on the unpopular midnight shift, including mandatory weekend shifts. But it was also several pay grades above entry level jobs and included at least eight hours of guaranteed overtime every week. So it was a great opportunity for newer employees that didn't have enough seniority to win other job bids to make some extra money. But the extra money didn't mean as much to me as the experience. Machine cleaning involved a great deal of machine operation as much of the equipment needed to be run or at least jogged at some point during the cleaning process. There was also a great deal of equipment disassembly required in most cleaning processes. So this served as an introduction to factory equipment operation and maintenance for me, something I ended up building an entire career on.

But anyway, back to my friend's party. I met a packaging mechanic from the previously mentioned plastics manufacturer. We both liked rock and roll, motorcycles and stock car races and quickly became friends. Soon, the conversation turned to careers. My new buddy had just received the biggest paycheck of his career after putting in 65 hours the previous week. And he wasn't shy about sharing the grand total of his weekly windfall with anyone willing to listen.

Then he started poking and prodding me, wanting to know what my salary was. It's not that I cared if he, or anyone else within hearing range, for that fact, knew what I made. I was every bit as proud of my salary as he was of his. I just didn't want to seem as if I was gloating because based on the information he supplied me, my salary was quite a bit higher than his, even though he was more than a couple of rungs higher than me on the manufacturing career ladder.

But as much as I tried to save my new-found friend from his overbearing curiosity, he refused to relent. So when I finally divulged the information, he so badly thought he wanted to hear, his once confident smile melted right of his face. Actually, he even got a little angry. The fact that I made almost $50 more, for the week, as a machine cleaner than he did as a mechanic seemed to infuriate him. I didn't have the heart to tell him that not only did I make $50 more than him, but I also worked 15 hours less than him.

So as much as my buddy originally thought he was satisfied with his job, he seemed to change his mind in a hurry when he met someone who worked for a truly good company. And as much as he seemed to enjoy working as a mechanic, every time I saw him after that night, he asked me if they were hiring machine cleaners where I worked. And I'm pretty sure, given the opportunity; he would have jumped ship in a heartbeat. That's the kind of loyalty good wages can buy for a company. But perhaps a better example would be, that's the kind of disloyalty sub-par wages purchase.

CHAPTER 20. A TALE OF TWO PACKERS: SUMMING IT ALL UP

Okay, another chapter down and I still haven't found my elusive con- clusion. But I think I've got it in my sights now. This wrap-up will re- quire a trip back in time to my team leader days when my department was at its height of using temporary employees.

With all the inexperienced temporary employees I had packing on lines, I needed more eyes on the floor. So I started thinking about the small number of regular employees I had been using to train the temps and started trying to think of ways to better utilize them. The first one who came to mind was an older lady named Margaret. Margaret was a 30-year veteran of the company, but not our plant. Our plant was located on the south side of Chicago. There was also a sister plant that was part of the original corporation on the west side. That plant got caught up in the consolidation efforts and was closed a few years prior to this. The employees at that plant were given several options to choose from for termination packages, including the opportunity to transfer to our plant. Margaret was one of about 50 people who chose to transfer.

Margaret brought something to my department that few others could. We had all learned to live with uncertainty brought on from the fear of a possible plant closure over the past few years. But Margaret carried around with her the reality of living through a plant closure that only 49 other people at that plant understood. And that was a driving force behind her commitment to quality. Indeed, Margaret must have had that drive to start with. She was too determined to have developed it over- night. But the fear of living through that scenario again pushed her to do everything in her power to try and avoid it.

So instead of having her continue to sit on a line with a temporary employee and show them the ropes, I turned her loose to weave in and out of the lines, helping and instructing wherever she could. And Margaret made her presence known. She was meticulous at spotting the smallest mistakes, much to the chagrin of many of the temporary employees who didn't share her enthusiasm for their jobs. They gave her dirty looks, mocked her, and occasionally even yelled at her—but none of that mattered. She remained relentless in her quest to make our department as mistake-free as possible, in spite of what anyone else thought. And that was a big help for me. If I had one sloppy, inexperienced packer, I could stand over them the majority of the shift and keep an eye on them until they got it right. If I had two, I could split my time between them and still be relatively effective. If I had three or four ... well, I could only be in so many places in one night.

Things worked so well with Margaret, I figured if one was good, two could only be better. My next most effective trainer was a young girl named Donna. Donna came in with the last batch of permanent new hires just before the flood of temporaries hit. So she was short on experience, but long on determination. I turned her loose with Margaret. And just like Margaret, Donna watched the inexperienced temporaries like a hawk and pointed out every little mistake. It was almost ironic, in a way.

They were polar opposites in their career aspects but almost like twins in their commitment to the company. Margaret had a clear view of retirement in sight. And after surviving one plant closure, her focus was clearly on doing everything to make sure this plant stayed open long enough for her to execute her exit strategy. Donna, on the other hand, was just beginning her journey and was anxious to make her mark. In many ways, she reminded me of myself back when I first started there. She was constantly looking around, asking questions, trying to learn as much as she could about the operation in general and always looking for opportunities to prove herself.

With Margaret on one side of the department and Donna on the other, I was far more confident in the quality level of the packages leaving our department. Some questioned my use of these ladies in this capacity, thinking maybe I was crossing some type of imagery line that should separate trainers from those with true management authority. A few even suggested I was using these ladies to do "my" job. My reply to them was simple enough: isn't that what an effective leader does? You identify the individual strengths of the members of your team and you utilize those strengths in a way that best supports the mission of the business. My department had a problem, and I found a solution. Was it the best possible solution to the problem? Absolutely not. But it may very well have been the best available solution at the time.

Then, one day, Margaret came into the office with tears welling up in her eyes. This wasn't the first time I saw her in this state. The first time I witnessed her watery eyes was when she came to me in confidence many months earlier to express her concerns over what she felt was an unacceptable quality level coming off many of the lines manned by temporary employees. But the teary eyes on that day seemed to gleam with determination and hope, while the teary eyes on this night had defeat written all over them.

"I can't do this anymore," Margaret said in a trembling voice, slightly louder than a whisper. The tone in her voice seemed to incorporate a myriad of emotions ranging from disappoint to disgust, surrender to defeat, and possibly even a twinge of embarrassment. She went on to explain that the hostility towards her on the floor was increasing among some of the younger temporaries and she was afraid, working nights, that someone might damage her car in the parking lot after dark in retaliation for what was beginning to be perceived as harassment. I could understand her concern. Many of the temporary employees the agency was sending us were from "questionable" areas of the city, or to put it bluntly, neighborhoods that were ridden with crime and gang violence. At least a few of our younger temporaries also displayed some "questionable" behaviors.

But although I believe her concerns for her car in the parking lot may have been part of the reason she was saying what she was saying, I think it was a small part at best. I think what Margaret was really trying to say is that she was tired—more like exhausted, actually. I couldn't say I blamed her. Trying to watch over four, five, maybe six people at time, attempting to catch every little mistake and offer constructive criticism that was often seen as annoying knit-picking was a frustrating—not to mention thankless—job. It wasn't completely thankless, of course. I certainly appreciated what she did, and tried to remember to tell her that every chance I got. But no one else did.

Training was considered a part of everyone's job. But I always seemed to have someone that didn't want to train people. I respected that— when I could. I would much rather have a cooperative trainer than an unwilling one, for obvious reasons. But with so many temporaries, and so few regulars, there were times when I had to force people to be trainers, rather they wanted to or not. But what I was asking Margaret to do was far beyond what her normal job duties called for. Not to mention, she had done far more than her fair share.

So I thanked her for all her effort, told her she had done an outstanding job that I deeply appreciated, and reassigned her to her old line where she could sit alone, meticulously picking out every little defect and take pride in knowing that she was doing all she could do to assure a maximum level of quality was rolling off her line. I hated to make that change. I really needed her to continue to do what she was doing. But the way I saw it, I really didn't have much of a choice. I was just thankful she did this for as long as she did. Luckily, I still had Donna to count on.

As I made these somewhat unusual changes in my department to accommodate the large amount of temporary employees, the company was taking similar steps in their own ways. First, they requested a fulltime on-site coordinator from the temporary agency so there was someone available at the plant to coordinate temporary employee activity all day. They eventually added supervisors from the temp agency on all shifts. The temps still reported directly to the company team leaders for their respective departments for day to day business. The supervisors from the temp agency basically checked at the beginning of the shifts to verify all temps had shown up and were where they were supposed to be. They also checked with the team leaders towards the end of the shift to see if there were any problems and coordinate how many temps each department needed for the next day. So basically they were glorified attendance takers for the most part, with a few other loosely defined duties added in. But the company seemed to think they served a purpose.

Personally, I saw it a little differently. I knew who was there and who was not before my department even hit the lines. So if I was missing a temp somewhere on a line, I was informing the temp supervisor of the absence, not the other way around. That is, unless the missing temp actually called into the temp supervisor ahead of time. But again, the temp supervisors weren't performing any tremendously helpful function by fielding these calls for us. I was always in the office at least 30 minutes prior to the start of the shift. And, of course, there was always someone from first shift in the office available to take a message for me before I arrived. The temps could have called into our office just as easily as they could call the temp supervisor—just as they used to do, before these supervisors were invented. In my eyes, they were more of a hindrance than a help.

One day I was away from the department for an extended period of time, searching the warehouse high and low for packaging materials that the computerized inventory system said were there while the material handler that was supposed to deliver them to my department swore they didn't exist. Without these materials, my department would come to a grinding halt, forcing an emergency changeover while also causing us to miss our case plan for that particular product by several hundred cases.

Fortunately, I was far more diligent in my search than the material handler and found the misplaced packaging materials several aisles from where the computer stated it was staged. This was just one example of emergency scenarios that sprung up constantly and forced me to abandon my department temporarily, depending on my well-trained operators, as well as motivated lower-level employees like Margaret and Donna to keep the department running in an orderly fashion.

Upon returning to the department, I was met by the temp supervisor who was waiting for me with some distressing news. She informed me that one of the temporaries had walked off the line and gone home, causing the line to be down for several minutes until she found another temp to man the line since I was nowhere to be found. She could have used the paging system to locate me. It could be heard throughout the entire warehouse as well as the plant. But she decided to handle the situation on her own instead, for whatever reason, and allowed the young woman to leave, even though she did not have the authority to do that. Like I said, more of a hindrance than a help.

I asked if the woman who had left was sick. "Nope," she replied in a quick and almost sarcastic tone. "She said she had to leave because if she stayed any longer she would end up punching Donna in the mouth."

My reply was as quick and direct as her answer. "Well, make sure she never comes back."

The temp supervisor seemed shocked by my immediate reaction, and she clearly viewed it as harsh. That was about the simplest, no-brainer decision I ever made in this job. For starters, she had walked off the job. That's always unacceptable. Secondly, she caused unnecessary downtime, another manufacturing no-no. And last but not least, she apparently threatened another employee with violence. Three strikes and you're out.

A day or two after this incident, the temp supervisor told me the on-site coordinator wanted me to come see him tomorrow. I asked her why, and she said he wanted to ask me to reconsider allowing the young lady who walked off the line to come back to the plant and work in a different department. I told her there was nothing he could say to change my mind, but she could tell him I'd come see him as soon as I got my shift started the next day and tell him that myself.

I even had precedent to back my decision up with, if need be. I actually had a temporary employee walk off a line early on when we first started using temps, long before the days of an on-site coordinator or these temp agency shift supervisors, when the temps dealt directly and exclusively with us. My investigation of the whole situation was abruptly interrupted, so to this day, I still don't know exactly what had happened.

I had a young girl, barely out of high school, who had been with me for months and was doing an outstanding job. She was extremely quiet and reserved. I knew almost nothing about her other than the fact that I never remember finding as much as a single defect packed on her line from my multiple in-department audits, and the operators all seemed to like her and never complained about her packing skills. And during her original training, with Margaret, no less, she was given a stellar report of being ready to be put on her own after just a few days—a feat accomplished by very few before, and even fewer since.

Then one day I was called over to her line, and the operator told me she had left. I pressed for more information but no one seemed to know where she went—or why. I quickly found a replacement to get the line back up and running, then paged the missing temp to my office. I paged her several more times over the next 15 minutes, then let it go and wrote her off as gone for whatever reason.

A few hours later, the missing temp walked into the office and requested a private, closed-door meeting with me to explain why she had left. I agreed, if for no other reason than curiosity, because in addition to her excellent performance record, her attendance record was every bit as impressive, so I knew something very out of the ordinary must have occurred to push her out the door.

Apparently, there was an issue brewing for the past few days between this young girl and some older female employees over attention she was getting from a certain older male employee. She was very evasive when it came to details, so evasive I didn't know if these other females were regular employees or other temps. I wasn't even sure if they were from my department or another one. But she was noticeably shaken, so I continued to press, hoping to eventually get some names. If someone in my department was creating a hostile work environment, I wanted to know about it. Another thought in the back of my mind was that, if for some reason this girl couldn't continue to work in my department, perhaps I could get one of the other team leaders to take her on. She was hard-working and dependable, traits not easy to find among the temps. If I could no longer benefit from her dedication because of some kind of personal conflict that made her too uncomfortable to remain in my department, why not pass those valuable resources on to another department in the plant?

What I didn't realize at the time, however, was this quiet and polite young lady had not returned alone. As I continued my probing, I heard a knock on the office door. I looked through the window and saw the shift coordinator peering in. He motioned me to come out to where he was. I excused myself and stepped out to see what he wanted.

"Did you have an employee from the temporary agency walk off the job tonight?" he asked.

"Yes, I'm talking to her right now, trying to determine what happened."

"Are you aware she came back with a small army and they're all at the back door right now?"

Of course my reply was a somewhat stunned "no."

"Come with me," he said with his hand already twisting the doorknob open. "I'll show you how to handle this."

He burst into the office and skipped any pleasantries like, "Hi, I'm the shift coordinator, is there a problem" and went straight to the heart of the matter.

"Who are all those people out there at the back door?"

"My friends," the young girl replied in her standard soft and almost sheepish tone.

"They here looking for Trouble?"

"No, sir."

"Then why are they here?"

"They drove me back here so I wouldn't have to take the bus. And now they're just waiting to see if I'm going to need a ride home or stay for the rest of the shift."

"Well, I hope that's the truth, because if they're here looking for trouble, I can guarantee you I'll have plenty for them. I've already called the police and they have a squad circling the neighborhood just waiting for me to call them back."

"There won't be any trouble, sir. I promise. They're just waiting for me, that's all."

With that, the shift coordinator seemed satisfied and motioned me to follow him back out the door. Once we were on the other side of the closed door, he glared at me briefly, and then finally spoke.

"I don't know what you think you're trying to accomplish in there but this should have been easy enough for you to figure out on your own without my help. She walked off the job. That's unacceptable under any circumstances. So why would you waste your valuable trying to find out why? And on top of that, she's obviously trying to pull off some kind of intimidation tactics with all those people out back. And if we ever even hint that we're willing to accept that kind of behavior, we'll really be in trouble. And last but certainly not least, she's only a temporary. We don't owe her any explanation. Just get rid of her and make damn sure she never comes back."

I must admit I was a little embarrassed after such a "you've got a lot to learn, rookie" type scolding. I actually had a minimum of three bosses. When the company went to the team leader format, the original supervisors, that still held rank over the team leaders, were renamed coaches. The coaches were seen as almost purely administrative with the team leaders carrying the bulk of the responsibility for the floor. In the early days of this transition, the coaches were responsible for training new team leaders and were slowly transitioned into other administrative, or depending on their backgrounds, sometimes engineering areas once a team leader was considered capable of running a department on their own. These transitions continued until there was one coach over an entire group of team leaders.

I was on second shift and just prior to this incident the original second shift supervisor, now dubbed my coach, had been moved to engineering and I was now running the shift solo. Technically, the business unit manager for our division, or the BUM, as we referred to him, was my ultimate boss. The old first shift supervisor was now the official coach for our department and he was my immediate boss. But, of course, since he was on first shift, and I was on second, our day to day interaction encompassed about an hour of face to face time, most of which I spent running around setting up for my shift while he was busy closing out his.

My number three boss was the second shift coordinator. They came and went fairly quickly over the years, either retiring or waiting their time out until being reassigned to first shift. But they all had one thing in common and that was that they all had very minimal impact on the way I operated my department. Most would walk through a maximum of one to two times a shift. If they saw me, they'd ask how everything was going, I would say fine, and they would walk away.

And that was actually far more contact than I had with my first shift coordinator. I almost never saw him. As a matter of fact, the first time I ever spoke face to face with him was that infamous conversation outside the office door the night my first temp walked off the job. Looking back, I probably didn't make the best first impression under the circumstances.

But anyway, I recanted that entire episode in my head while heading to the on-site temp coordinator's office the next day, just in case I decided to cite it as precedent. But I didn't really anticipate discussing too much of anything. My case was open and shut. I was planning on walking into the office, giving him maybe a minute at best to plead his case before I told him in no uncertain terms, I wasn't changing my mind.

On my way to his office, however, I ran into him along with the temp supervisor and they were both heading away from their office. When he saw me, he pointed in the other direction and informed me we were meeting in the employee training room. He also told me the head of personnel and a few other people were already there waiting for us. I didn't have a clue what in the world was happening, but suddenly I felt a little like a lamb being led to slaughter.

As we rounded the corner, it just so happened that we ran into the shift coordinator. He had just been assigned to the shift a few weeks ago and my contact with him in this position to this point had been almost nonexistent. But, fortunately for me, I knew him well. I had first met him when I was stacking cases on a line and he was the lead man. That was roughly 20 years ago. And since that time, I had worked for him here and there in several different capacities over the years after he became a supervisor. We had always gotten along well and he knew I always did a good job.

So the light bulb immediately went off in my head—a possible ally. He said "hi," and continued walking. But before he could get too far away I grabbed him and said, "I'm not sure exactly where we're going—or why—but I think I might need you to come with me." He started following, and I did the best I could to explain the little bit I actually understood of what was happening.

When we walked in, the room appeared to be set up in a very deliberate fashion. At the front of the room was a short table running north and south with a single chair where the personnel director was sitting all alone: The judge. Then there was a long table set up running east and west with several chairs that seemed to have very specific placements. Sitting in the first chair, closest to the personnel director, was the temp girl that had walked out a couple nights ago: The witness/victim. There was a small gap in between her chair and the next two. I can't even remember who was sitting there; I think I recall someone else from our personnel department and maybe someone from the temp company's home office: Stenographers, perhaps? There was another small gap then two more chairs. The on-site coordinator and temp supervisor immediately made themselves comfortable there: The prosecution team. That left just one available chair in the room, sitting at another short north and south table facing straight at the personnel director's chair, which was obviously meant for me: The defendant.

The people already in the room seemed a little surprised to see the shift coordinator walk in with me. Obviously, this whole kangaroo court set-up was supposed to be a blind-side ambush to catch me off guard. And for the most part they did. Even though the on-site coordinator probably tipped his hand a little too early by telling me where we were going and who was there waiting, the fact that I quickly decided to involve the shift coordinator as an ally was far more a coincidental fluke than any kind of well-thought-out, quick thinking on my part.

So they pulled up another chair next to mine for my boss and began the...well...I don't even know what to call whatever it was happening here—proceedings maybe? My boss made a comment almost immediately, and then at least a couple more times throughout this farce, that he was upset that he was hearing about this issue now for the first time since it appeared by the way it was being handled to be a major issue. I originally took this comment as a dig on me, thinking he was referring to the fact that I didn't bring it to his attention that I was having issues with temporaries in my department. But that wasn't how I did business. And I was pretty sure he was aware of that. I was a big boy and I handled my own problems in my department, as I was always told I should.

Coaches, shift coordinators—whatever you wanted to call them—were suppose to be the next level you go to when the problem becomes too big to handle on your own. I made it very clear to everyone I reported to early on that I had several reservations about possible quality impacts that could arise utilizing temporaries as packers, which, in a nutshell, were also our final inspectors. Then, when it became clear that was the way it was going to be—like it or not—I did the best I could with what I had to work with.

As this, whatever it was, continued, I began starting to realize that my boss' comments about not being properly informed of this issue were probably directed more at the personnel people than me. And for good reason. This was far from the first time my procedures or actions were questioned. And not just mine, all the team leaders and coaches had grievances filed against them for one thing or another eventually. But what was happening now was as far away as you can get from standard operating procedure.

As I mentioned early on in the first chapters of this book, this plant had a very successful grievance procedure program that had a high employee satisfaction rate. And most grievances were settled in the first or second phases, long before anyone from personnel was even involved. But as much as this process usually worked out well for the employees, the process was also fair for the most part to management. We were notified almost immediately when a formal grievance was filed against us. And we were notified well in advance of any pending official meetings to gather information so we had time to collect our thoughts and present our side of the story clearly. A management person's immediate supervisor, usually a coach in the case of a team leader or the BUM in the case of a coach, were also made immediately aware of the situation and would usually discuss the issue with their underling to find out what happened, and perhaps even offer advice on how to proceed once the official procedure started.

But all that was thrown out the window for this one. We were apparently riding on the "bypass the system express" a high-speed, nonstop, newly invented grievance procedure designed especially for the temporary agency's on-site coordinator that went from 0 to phase four of the standard grievance procedure, a meeting with the plant manager and/or personnel director, in approximately one-second or less, without as much as informing the passengers of the destination prior to boarding.

It was obvious somebody (or some bodies) wanted to either humiliate or intimidate me into changing the way I ran my department and lower my quality standards to make things easier for the temps. That was something I was not prepared to tolerate—and I didn't give a damn who was sitting at the head of the table at this point. I had two basic management philosophies I always adhered to. They were straight forward, went hand in hand and were heard by my crew on numerous occasions. And they also applied equally to regular, as well as, temporary employees. The first was as simple as you can get, "do not embarrass me, and I won't have to embarrass you."

I couldn't have made my expectations any clearer than that. But to clarify even further, I would elaborate from time to time with specific examples. For instance, I would tell my crew things like, there is nothing embarrassing about an operator or packer coming to tell me they just discovered defects on their line and they think some of them may have been packed and sent to the wrappers before they caught the defects. That just showed they were doing their jobs. And there was nothing embarrassing in these same instances about me going out to warehouse to spot check pallets of cases run on those lines, discovering some defects, and placing a couple of hours worth of production on hold for further evaluation. That just showed I was doing my job.

If we are all just standing around and going through the motions, allowing the department to operate on autopilot, on the other hand, and quality control comes through, identifies the same defects we should be finding on our own on multiple lines and places an entire shift's worth of production on hold, well, that would be extremely embarrassing. Just for the record, nothing even close to that ever happened on my shift. And I intended to keep it that way.

My second managerial philosophy dealt more with what happens when people may consider challenging my first philosophy. And that was "if you do your job properly, my job is easy and most of the time, you won't even know I'm here. If you refuse to do your job, on the other hand, then you leave me no choice but to do mine. And we are both going to be made to be uncomfortable."

Part "A" of this was simple enough. Do your job—and do it right. That not only included high quality standards but an array of other "must dos" as well. Like working safely, keeping your work area neat and tidy, cooperating and getting along with co-workers and last but not least, either making your daily production quota or properly and accurately documenting your downtime to explain why production was not made. For employees who did this, I would stroll by their lines several times a shift, say hi, maybe take a minute to ask them how things were going, and then walk away. Basically, the same treatment I received from the various shift coordinators over the years when they made an appearance in my department.

I would never notice if they took a little longer for break, snuck in an extra smoke break or two, were chewing gum or were doing an inadequate job of concealing a magazine on the line that they apparently thought was hidden out of sight. Why would I notice these things? It all came down to philosophy one, they weren't embarrassing me, so I had no reason to embarrass them.

Unfortunately, this philosophy didn't work with many of the temporaries. There were multiple situations that could have resulted in my being embarrassed every shift. And these were only the situations I knew about. Who knows what I possibly wasn't seeing while trying to monitor eight lines at one time.

I didn't like having to do many of the things I was now forced to do. Standing over people, hounding and knit-picking, was about as far from my preferred management style as you could get. And asking other people to do these things with me was something I was even less comfortable about. But as I clearly stated in my philosophy two, when I was forced to do my job because other people refused to do theirs, we were both going to be made uncomfortable. And many of the temporaries were not doing their jobs properly so not only was I made to do things that made me uncomfortable but I was also forced to make other people uncomfortable as well.

And that philosophy is apparently what landed me here. As these proceedings continued, it was clear the outcome was predetermined. I was going to be found guilty of picking on the temporary employees. This was just a smokescreen to make it appear as if the question had yet to be answered. If this wasn't clear at the onset, it definitely came into focus when I started getting leading questions like, "were you aware temporary employees were being harassed in your department?"

To which I gave direct and deliberate answers like, "no one was being harassed in my department. There were, however, heightened in-department conducted quality audits authorized by me in a direct response to an unacceptable increase in defects being packaged and sent to the wrapper area as opposed to being removed and scrapped on the packing line as required. These audits were conducted randomly across all lines in the department regardless of who the packers were and no one person, or persons, were singled out for heightened scrutiny."

To which my boss just gave a slight tilt of his head in my direction, while his eyes opened wide and the corners of his mouth turned up slightly, stopping just short of a full-blown smile, as if he was sending a nonverbal statement similar to "good answer."

Since it appeared I was never going to get a chance to plead my case, I made my own chance and addressed the young temp on my own, questioning her as to why she just left as opposed to coming to me to give me an opportunity to rectify the situation. Her answer went something like, "because you would just be on her side, Clyde. You're always on her side."

I would be "on her side?" Were we in a meeting room of a major corporation or the principal's office at the local high school? If it wasn't bad enough she had already walked off the job on me, caused my department unnecessary downtime and apparently threatened one of my team members, but now she was also adding insult to injury by insinuating I couldn't be objective and impartial while investigating a dispute between two employees. The only reason I even brought this whole subject up was to shine a little light back on the fact that this whole scenario was being played out because this woman had walked off the job, a "should have been" important piece of the puzzle that everyone else was apparently willing to sweep under the rug.

I had originally stated there was no excuse for ever walking off a job. Based on some of my past experiences since this time, however, I would like to amend that statement slightly. The only legitimate excuse for walking off a job is if you are being told to do something illegal, immoral, unethical or dangerous. The night I was told to move slot machines across land in South Carolina, then found out it was technically illegal, I had a legitimate excuse to walk off the job. The multiple times we had to evacuate the room at the poultry plant due to dangerous CO_2 levels, then were sent right back in without the problem first being corrected, we all had a legitimate excuse to walk off the job. Or the mornings we were forced into the plant to set-up while choking on parasitic acid, or when we were sent into the spiral freezer without proper thermal protective clothing, or when we had to run the dicers without working E-stops... But having a disagreement with another employee and "thinking" the person supervising the area wouldn't treat you fairly without even giving him a chance, is not a reason to walk off a job.

I found myself wondering, for just a moment, if this episode for the temp in question, could compare to my coder experience with The Enforcer. I was well aware of the fact that Donna could be a little... well... let's just say abrasive, for lack of better word, at times when she felt someone was not putting sufficient effort into doing their jobs properly. But I let it go because I also knew from my own experience dealing with temporary employees that a little tough talk was the only way to get the attention of some of the least motivated of this largely unreliable workforce. But I also realized it had to be kept within certain reasonable limits and I did wonder if perhaps Donna had taken this incident a step too far.

But after just a little more thought, I realized that would be like comparing apples to oranges. What kind of recourse could I have possibly had? Where could I have possibly gone for help? The Intimidator? He was just as bad as and at times worse than, The Enforcer. The maintenance manager? Yeah, I'm sure he would have been a big help. He was standing right next to me the whole time this was happening and never said a word in my defense. I did have a supervisor, but seeing how the maintenance manager witnessed this whole fiasco and didn't say a word, what could I expect the supervisor to do?

This woman, on the other hand, had plenty of recourse. First and foremost, she should have come to me. And if she really felt she couldn't get a fair evaluation from me, she should have gone to my boss, the shift coordinator, and explained her dilemma to him. And last but not least, had the temp supervisor acted like a true supervisor, she would have persuaded the woman not to leave and got either me or the shift coordinator involved immediately.

Then there was the apparently completely overlooked little subject of alleged intimidation this woman committed. According to what the temporary supervisor told me, this woman specifically said that if she stayed any longer, she was going to punch Donna in the mouth. If that wasn't a threat, I don't know what else you could call it. And all the team leaders and coaches had just been through extensive workplace violence training where we were instructed to take even the slightest hint of possible violence or intimidation seriously and act immediately.

But that whole segment of this incident was never brought up. I really should have brought it up. But I was too busy defending myself and was given very little leeway to direct the conversation. I was obviously the one on trial here, not the temporary employee who walked off the job.

The fact that the threat of a "punch in the mouth" never became an issue made me wonder if the whole thing ever really even happened. I started wondering, did she really say that, or was that language just the best way the temporary supervisor thought she could get my attention? It was that exact language that made me react so quickly. And now I was wondering if the whole thing wasn't just political theater, again in an attempt to pressure me to adjust the way I operated my department.

And looking back now, if that was the case, I should have called her on her bluff. Right there, right then and most importantly, right in front of my boss, her boss, the personnel director and everyone else in the room. If this was a real threat that had been made, it should have been a big part of this whole discussion. And if it turned out there had not been any actual threat made, it should have been an even bigger part of the conversation as to why I was told there was.

But I guess all of this never really entered my mind. And it's easy to look back now and say it certainly should have. But as long and drawn out as this story has become, on paper, when it was happening in real time, it was a whirlwind. I was taken completely by surprise, and it felt like the whole room against me, which certainly didn't help to make me think clearly.

The on-site coordinator from the temporary agency, who seemed to be given the majority of the floor time, kept referring to a pendulum analogy. He kept talking about anytime there was any friction between a temporary and any regular employee, the pendulum only swung in one direction, the direction of the regular employee, which only made sense to me. I wanted to see the temporary employees treated fairly as much as anyone. I wanted to see everyone treated fairly. And I wanted to see everyone happy. Happy employees were far more easily motivated than disgruntled ones. But when problems occasionally arose between regular employees and temporary ones, I also had the good business sense to realize which one of these groups were more important to the overall success of the company. The regular employees were the past, present and presumably the future of this company. The temporaries, on the other hand, were the company's present at best, with many here today and gone tomorrow.

My adversary from the temporary agency, however, had a slightly different opinion. His argument seemed to cling to the suggestion that the company had become so dependent on temporary employees as an instrumental part of their workforce that they better start finding ways to pacify some of the unrest mounting on the temporary employees side of the equation or the agency might not be able to continue to supply temporaries in the amounts the plant required. In addition to his pendulum analogy, he also started throwing around the phrase "win one" implying if this business relationship was going to remain successful between the plant and the temporary agency, it was important that the temporaries could, at least occasionally, win one every now and then against a regular employee.

Again, I thought his rhetoric was insane from purely a business point of view. To say you are more concerned with appeasing a temporary employee that may be gone before the dust from the incident settles than risking the possibility of alienating a permanent employee with a solid work history that may be with the company for 30+ years is just plain ludicrous. But again, from his perspective I'm sure this made sense. His was a numbers game. As I stated before the temp agency's profit margin was driven solely by quantity and had no dependence whatsoever on quality. So they had everything to gain and nothing to lose by sending us employees that might not live up to our quality expectations. They were compensated for the total number of hours that employee spent in our plant rather we were completely satisfied, only somewhat satisfied, or completely dissatisfied with that employee's performance.

Apparently, the personnel director bought into his philosophy over mine, though, because the young woman was allowed to come back on the same shift working in a different department. I knew the team leader that was now in charge of the temp that caused all this mayhem well. He was a personal friend I had known for many years, as was the case for me with the majority of the other team leaders, and we shared many a lunches together at the same table in the cafeteria after this incident. But I made it a point never to mention this incident to him, or even as much as mention her name, in fear that if the word got out somehow that I spoke to him about her, I may be accused by our personnel department of trying to soil her reputation or somehow be attempting to "get even" with her.

I also avoided having any contact with her, as well. That was easy enough for the most part with her working two departments over from mine. But there were rare occasions I couldn't avoid when I'd bump into her in the cafeteria or walk past her in the hallway on our way to or from lunch. In which cases I would avoid direct eye contact as much as possible but also made sure I always delivered a simple but polite hello. To which she would reply back in the same short but polite manner and we would both continue on our separate ways.

I tried not to let it bother me whenever I saw her in the plant. I must admit, however, I always wondered what my original shift coordinator, who "taught me" how to handle the situation when a temporary employee walked off the job, would have thought of this whole fiasco every time I walked past her. But for the most part, I was just glad this whole episode was over—or so I thought.

A good week, perhaps even two, after I thought this whole three-ring circus had been put to rest, the shift coordinator walked into my office right after the start of the shift. He informed me he had to see Donna before the end of the shift. Of course, I inquired as to why. He then stated personnel wanted Donna spoken to about the incident with the temporary employee and if he didn't do it, they would.

I immediately protested. I told him again, as I had before, that Donna was simply carrying out my instructions. So if he felt he needed to reprimand anyone, it needed to be me and I would then take the matter up with personnel on my own behalf.

He, in return, immediately tried to calm me down. He assured me this would be a casual conversation, officially documented as a non-disciplinary record of discussion, which means it does not count against the employee as a disciplinary issue under the progressive disciplinary system. This assurance did ease my mind somewhat. But I still wasn't satisfied. So I told him I wanted to be present at the meeting, as well. He agreed. I then informed him in no uncertain terms, just to make sure he realized that I was not planning to attend this meeting as an ally for him. He chuckled slightly and said something like, "I wouldn't have it any other way" as he walked out the door.

I waited a couple of hours then took Donna off to the side to explain what was going to happen around the end of shift. I wanted to give her a few hours to collect her thoughts as opposed to being caught in a total blindside like I was when this whole seemingly endless nightmare began. She appeared shocked, not to mention noticeably upset, when I explained the situation. And her reaction was completely understandable considering she had done nothing other than follow her immediate supervisor's instructions. Perhaps she followed my instructions a little too well and took things to extremes. But even if that was the case, she was still simply following my instructions nonetheless.

When the shift was about to wind down my boss and I both sat down with Donna for a closed door meeting in the office. I started the meeting off by reiterating one final time that I felt Donna had done nothing more than what I asked her to do and stated I stood behind her 100-percent. Then I turned the floor over to my boss. If I had to describe the way he handled this situation in only one word, that word would be masterfully. He basically made the whole conversation about how certain well-meaning personality traits could be viewed by other people as harsh, and maybe even at times overbearing. He really did a great job, in my opinion, of keeping the message focused on personality conflicts and steered completely away of any accusations of any wrongdoing on Donna's part. I don't believe he could have handled it anymore tactfully.

But, of course, Donna didn't see it that way. She had disgust written all over her face the entire time. And I can't say I blame her. This whole episode should have never been escalated to anywhere near the level it had reached.

I don't know if I completely realized it at the time, but this was my first personal experience of getting caught in the crossfire of a company attempting to pander to a source of cheap labor.

And again I have to ponder the question, what is it about these temporary employees a company considers cheap? From what I had been told, we were considered a premium company for the employees from the temporary agency. This meant, quite simply, that we paid more by the hour to the temps than the majority of the companies in the area using the same temp agency, most of which paid their temps minimum wage. But this also meant we paid more to the temp agency per hour for every temp we used. I was told we were paying our temps somewhere around $7.00 to $8.00 per hour. I was also told the temp agency made close to, and sometimes as much as each employee, per hour. So this translated into roughly double that hourly rate as the cost to the company, which, ironically, was more than we paid our lowest level permanent employees that would be doing the jobs these temps were filling in on. They made roughly $13.00 per hour at the time.

So the labor costs for using temporary employees versus hiring regular employees was a break even venture at best, perhaps even costing slightly more. So the only cost savings were in the areas of administrative costs and benefits. I'm sure the savings in benefits costs were substantial, but those benefits costs could also be worth their weight in gold in the amount of employee loyalty and satisfaction they could buy. I may have originally taken this job for the money, but it was the health insurance, 401K plan, paid holidays and accumulating vacation time that kept me there for all those years.

The most ironic part, perhaps, about this whole scenario was that the company and I both had the same end goal in sight. We both wanted to find ways to make the temps feel at home, which in turn would hopefully make them more productive. But the paths we had chosen to try and get there were miles apart.

We were starting to use a fair amount of temporary employees prior to the last batch of new hires that were brought in. I had a few temps that had been with me long enough to prove they were reliable and I was also satisfied with their job performance. One in particular had proven himself far above the others. So when the company announced they were going to hire some new employees, I wrote him what I considered to be an outstanding letter of recommendation. I also wrote very good recommendations for two or three other temps that I felt had proven they would make good permanent employees. Much to my surprise, none of these temps were hired, even though they already had experience in the plant and a recommendation from their immediate supervisor.

There was one more round of hiring done at the plant before I left. This time I wrote my favorite temp a letter of recommendation that was nothing short of spectacular. And to make sure it wasn't overlooked again, I hand delivered the letter to the personnel department myself as opposed to giving it to him to turn in with his application. I also wrote recommendations for any temps working in my department that I felt had sufficiently proven themselves to be reliable and capable of doing the job. These recommendations weren't nearly as good as the one I hand delivered to personnel, but they should have definitely been considered good enough to get someone hired, especially considering they came from a direct supervisor from the company. I don't remember the exact number of temps I recommended but it was somewhere around three or four in addition to the one I delivered the personal recommendation for.

This time my number one recommendation was at least hired, but the rest were still not. So the way I saw it, I did more than my fair share to take care of the deserving temporary employees. I may have been one of the strongest critics of lazy, irresponsible temps that didn't want to do their jobs properly, but I was also probably the staunchest supporter of those who demonstrated true commitment. In my opinion, rewarding the top performing temps with an opportunity to become permanent employees with full benefits and a big raise was the best possible way to motivate these temps to do the best job they could possibly do day after day.

But I can't take credit for inventing this philosophy. It was the same one the plant had used for decades, long before I even came along. Offer people good pay, adequate benefits, fair treatment and reasonable job security and they will be willing to make a long term commitment to the company. That was the philosophy I was raised on from the time I started with this company straight out of high school. And that was the same winning philosophy I felt could motivate the temporary employees. The company's new and improved philosophy for motivating the temporary employees, however, appeared to be to let the temps "win one" every now and then over a permanent employee.

My experience having my department overrun by temporary employees was relatively short-lived in retrospect to my long career at that plant—barely more than a blip on the radar screen, actually. But it was certainly memorable to say the least.

Part of the reason there wasn't more urgency placed on the quality issues the temporaries brought to my department may have had something to do with the fact that these jobs were going away. (I specified department rather than shift because it was not only my shift that had issues with the temps. I just had more issues than first and third shifts because I happened to be running the least desirable shift in the eyes of the regular employees which translated into having the most vacancies to fill, which also, of course, translated into having to use the largest number of temporaries). We were in the final planning stages of replacing eight outdated packaging lines that required manual hand-packing with four brand new, state of the art, high-speed automatic packing lines.

Once this upgrade was completed, my job became fairly easy again. I reverted back to my "don't embarrass me and I won't have to embarrass you" scenario. These new lines made everyone's lives easier. Not only were they a lot faster than the old lines but they were also almost completely defect free when operated properly. So I spent the majority of my nights from that point on in the office pushing papers or working on the computer and again depended on my crew to do their jobs, and do them right. And they liked having me in the office and out of sight as opposed to constantly on the floor and under their feet, so they did just that. And that, in my humble opinion, is exactly how a department—any department, regardless of industry or size—should run. When "the boss" has to stand in the middle of the department for the entire shift breathing down everyone's necks to make sure things get done properly the company is probably more at fault than the people. There is something wrong somewhere in the company's philosophy. Either the people on the floor are not being properly trained, or they are not being paid enough to be properly motivated, or the management policies of the company are so barbaric people are deliberately under-performing in retaliation, or last but not least, the company is just outright hiring the wrong people.

In the case of my issues with the temporaries, it was at least a little of all of the above. The pay was a no-brainer. Of course none of these temps were going to be motivated by their pay, especially when the company posted all open jobs, along with pay rates, on bulletin boards for all to see and the temps realized they were being forced to do jobs permanent employees didn't want to do for just a little over half of what a permanent employee would have been paid. As for the Training? Well, I did the best I could with that. But when you have a limited amount of qualified trainers to work with and a never ending revolving door of new people to be trained, someone is going to fall through the cracks somewhere. And that goes directly back to the self-induced problems caused by hiring the wrong people to start with. Some of these temps were good, but many sought work through a temporary agency because they were considered unhirable for one reason or another by permanent employers. So should it be a surprise that they may not meet our quality expectations?

To take this a step further, the majority of the problems at the poultry plant were caused by having the wrong people in the wrong places as well. Let's start with the masses in the production crew. Uneducated, illiterate people who are not even capable of speaking the language of the country they live and work in, whose most desirable traits in the eyes of an employer are that they work really fast, work very cheaply and are easy to intimidate are never going to be capable of being trusted to keep a department running efficiently without being constantly and consistently monitored.

As for the management staff, if the only way you think you can keep a workforce operating at maximum efficiency is to constantly berate, belittle, intimidate, threaten and coerce them into compliance, then you obviously lack the people skills necessary to be an effective manager and chose the wrong line of work. Not to mention the fact that your mother obviously never taught you the golden rule. Oh sure, they'll toe the line when you're in the room because they fear you. But as soon as you're not looking they're going to try and find a way to get even because although they may fear you, they equally hate you. And when they finally reach the level of frustration where they hate you more than they fear you there's no telling where that anger may take them.

Then there was the maintenance department, the one place this company absolutely had the right people. If there was only one thing I can say this company did do right, it was that they assembled a crew of experienced maintenance people that cut their teeth on factory floors of some of the most successful food manufacturers in the world. Unfortunately, this "right" group of maintenance people were sandwiched in between the "wrong" group of production workers that didn't posses the skills, or even the basic command of the country's language , for that fact, to run this facility efficiently and the "wrong" group of managers that constantly blamed the maintenance department for every problem in the process without ever showing enough respect for the collective experience of this department to allow them the opportunity to offer suggestions for improvement. So needless to say, the "right" maintenance people quickly got discouraged and started leaving one by one until only an 18 year-old kid straight out of high school and myself were the only ones left. These highly experienced maintenance people were quickly replaced with anyone that knew which end of a screwdriver the handle was on that were willing to work for $10 per hour and it wasn't long before this company had the wrong people in every area of operation. Yet upper management just couldn't understand why they couldn't seem to get this place operating at maximum efficiency.

I thought I learned a lot about managing people in difficult situations from my experience managing the temporary employees at that first factory. But it wasn't until I moved to Myrtle Beach that I really discovered the devastation low wages and insufficient benefits could deliver to a workforce. And it wasn't until I worked in the poultry industry that I truly witnessed what it was like to treat a certain group of workers as second class citizens.

I know times have changed. And I realize we are now competing in a global economy. I'm not going to even attempt to delve into all the political ramifications of this new economy. I'll leave that for the political experts. But I will concede that it is only natural for some changes to have to come about due to the new global manufacturing environment. But it appears we are now actually engaged in a full-blown war for our manufacturing jobs. It started with Japan and Taiwan, was soon joined by Mexico and has now spread to China and India. And these are just the major players. There are several other minor competitors waging war against us for our manufacturing base as well.

But one thing I do know, we could have chosen several winnable fronts to fight this battle against them on. We could have fought them with innovation instead of sharing it with them. No one could have ever beaten us on that front. We certainly could have fought them with quality. There's no way anyone will ever convince me that a bunch of uneducated peasants being paid 50¢ per-day in any third-world country could produce something of higher quality than a bunch of hard-working, blue-collar American factory workers. And with our experience combined with our innovation, I'd be willing to bet dollars to doughnuts we could out-produce those peasants as well.

But with all this playing in our favor, where did we choose to try and compete with them? In price—the one battlefield there is no way we can win on. And even when an American manufacturer like the poultry plant I worked in wins a small battle in this unwinnable war by continuing to do business in this country by adopting third-world manufacturing practices, the American people still lose.

Afterthoughts

When I started working in Myrtle Beach, I joked about writing a book. But then I would just chuckle and say I would have to bill it as fiction, because no one that has ever worked for a decent company would believe it. I even dedicated one of my magazine columns to the pathetic wages and unrealistic employer expectations during the off tourist season when the entertainment scene was slow. In that piece I coined the phrase "Move-to-Myrtle Beach-itis" to describe how so many people come to Myrtle Beach one time on vacation, instantly fall in love with the beach atmosphere and decide they want to live there, without doing any career research. That may have also been the first time I used the so sad but unfortunately true phrase, "Myrtle Beach, a great place to live, but you wouldn't want to work there." That column received a fair amount of comments and feedback, and it was all positive. That was my first clue that my career experiences might actually hold some entertainment value.

Then I migrated to the poultry industry, with all their sweatshop management tactics, third-world manufacturing practices and illegal workforces, and I realized I *had* to write a book.

At first, I thought these different career paths had little to do with one another. But as I started thinking the whole concept through as three separate, unrelated events, I realized this was one cohesive story from start to finish.

I had several purposes in mind when I first started this project. First, of course, was entertainment value. I write with the goal in mind that people will actually enjoy reading what I have written. I also hope management figures in industry, potential future ones as well as current, will value this work as an instruction manual: how to, and more importantly how *not* to motivate a workforce.

And, of course, I wrote this book as an information guide. People have a right to hear different sides of the illegal-immigration debate and other issues. And they certainly are not getting the workman's side from the mainstream media or political leaders.

Case in point. Not too long ago I heard a news story about an immigration raid at a meat processing plant, probably in Nebraska. The main focus of the story was not the fact that illegal immigrants were being employed at this particular company, nor did any of the so-called news stories I heard question company officials about the many illegal immigrants found in the plant. What was the actual story line all the news agencies focused on? There was a report that some Americans were heard cheering while the illegal immigrants (mostly Hispanic, for the record) were being escorted out by ICE.

The assumption by the America-bashing mainstream media, of course, was that the cheering employees were all big, bad, Hispanic-hating, racists. We all know Americans hate Hispanics. Just ask any open-borders advocates; they'll tell you all about it. Or better yet, ask any politician up for reelection in a district with a Hispanic population, even a small one. They'll back up the open-borders advocate on that one.

So there could be no other possible reason for some people at this plant to cheer at the site of this raid other than unbridled hatred and blatant racism, right? Wrong! Perhaps the cheers were in support of the federal government finally doing a very small part of a very much neglected job. Or maybe, the cheers were actually more like jeers directed at the company, kind of like an in-your-face, company, "you finally got what you deserve." Perhaps the legal employees envisioned a possible end to tyrannical management tactics if the company was forced to hire legal residents to replace these illegals and were cheering for that. Based on my own experiences, this thought would have made me cheer. Others could have been cheering at the prospect that some of their unemployed neighbors, friends and family members might actually be able to get a job at the plant if the illegal workers were leaving.

Then, of course, I can also think of some reasons that could cause these employees to cheer that may have been geared directly at the illegal immigrants. But they have nothing to do with racism. If these Hispanic immigrants were anything like the hundreds of Hispanic immigrants I worked side by side with for two years, very few—if any—spoke English. And the thought of no longer having to deal with the frustration, not to mention the danger of having to work around this equipment with people you can't communicate with is something else I would cheer about. That's not racism, that's just old-fashioned common sense. People who cannot effectively communicate with one another cannot effectively work together. Liberals (or anyone else, for that fact) who believe this is not an issue or a problem have obviously never dealt with it in real life.

And while we're on the subject, let me let you in on a little secret. Many middle class Americans have considerable animosity towards Hispanics who come here illegally and take what were traditionally blue collar, middle class jobs, for peanuts and no benefits. But again, it has nothing to do with the fact that they are Hispanic. It has everything to do with the fact that they are dragging down the wage base and destroying decent jobs. If this whole fiasco continues unchecked much longer, they will eventually destroy the middle class. That's not racism, that's just basic economics.

When I was 19 years old, I bought my first brand new car, on a factory worker's salary. At the age of 22, I got married for the first time, to another factory worker. We lived in a nice apartment and both drove late model vehicles. We also averaged two vacations a year to places like Disney World, Yellowstone Park and Niagara Falls and still managed to put a little money in the bank every week, all on factory workers' salaries.

I ended up divorced and living in an apartment alone. After several years of throwing money away on rent, I bought a two flat so I could live in one apartment and rent out the other. And I purchased this building solely from my factory worker's salary. I actually was convinced to go into the rental business on the side by coworkers who had found moderate to very lucrative success in this area, and many of them were legal immigrants.

Some years later I got remarried, to a wonderful woman with four children, and needed something bigger than my two bedroom apartment. I sold that two flat for a modest profit and bought a beautiful, four-bedroom, three-bathroom home with an attached garage, full, finished basement and a large, fenced in yard, all on a factory worker's salary.

I compiled this laundry list not to "toot my own horn" but to illustrate a point. Once upon a time a hard-working, blue-collar factory worker (as well as construction laborers, landscapers and other workers in areas that are now dominated by illegal immigrants) could make a decent living in this country. But as more and more companies hire illegal immigrants who are willing to accept wages far below that necessary to support the lifestyle of an average American, these opportunities for the Average Joe blue-collar American continue to dwindle away.

How are these illegal immigrants able to survive in America on such deflated wages, you may wonder? For starters, they drive old, dilapidated vehicles (many times vans that are purchased and shared by more than one family) with bald tires, cracked windshields, leaking and/or burning every fluid required to keep an engine running; and judging by what I saw around the poultry plant, it would be safe to assume many of them get by with even less.

And how about living quarters? It's no secret that many Hispanics live with multiple families crammed into small, single family homes. A house two doors down from mine in Myrtle Beach was rented to a group of Hispanic men for a couple of years. This home was perhaps a little smaller than the three-bedroom home that felt cramped for my family (two adults, four teenagers and a small child). Five to six cars were parked between the driveway and the front yard of the house these Hispanic men lived in at any given time. And based on the traffic I saw going in and out of that house on a daily basis, there must have been a dozen or more adults living in there. I've also heard stories of illegals working opposite 12-hour shifts so they could share beds in what amounted to no more than bunkhouses.

The legal European immigrants I worked with in the 1970s and 1980s were compensated well enough to buy apartment buildings and become landlords in addition to their manufacturing careers, while the illegal Hispanic immigrants working in manufacturing and other fields in the 21st century are lucky if they make enough money to pay rent. How's that for being treated like second class citizens? Where is their American dream? These people are being sought out by many American employers for the sole purpose of paying them less than they would have to pay Americans to do the same jobs. That's discrimination in its most basic definition.

Yet there seems to be no outcry from the liberal open-borders crowd in protest of the way these immigrants are being taken advantage of. They'll march in the thousands to protest any potential enforcement of our immigration laws as "racism" but seem disinterested in any debate over the "true discrimination" these illegal immigrants face every day on workroom floors across the country by being paid less and treated worse than the average American worker.

How are unskilled and low-skilled American workers supposed to compete with immigrants willing to work extremely hard and long, often in horrendous conditions, for extremely little? They can't, of course... that is unless they are willing to live in the same squalor and conditions. And that, ladies and gentlemen, will trigger the beginning of the end for the middle class in this country.

If these American companies that prey on desperate, illegal labor are allowed to continue and grow unrestricted for much longer, before you know it everyone is this country, including those born here and those here legally but who do not qualify to be a doctor, lawyer, or corporate big-wig, will be standing on a street corner holding a "will work for food" sign. We are on our way to quickly becoming a Third-world nation of haves and have-nots, where the have-nots will be literally enslaved by the haves. You will either own the construction company or toil away on a construction site from dawn to dusk before driving home to a house you share with another family, in a vehicle you co-own with two or three other coworkers. You will either be a corporate executive isolated from the have-nots behind the walls of a gated community, or you will work two full-time jobs just to be able to afford to live among the have-nots in far less pleasant conditions than blue collar workers enjoy today. You will either be part of the upper management staff at the local factory or you will, in essence, become a slave working on the floors of that factory.

Yet, with all this at stake, all the politicians and the mainstream media seem to want to talk about is how we will be viewed as racists if we secure our borders or deport people who have broken our laws. And that is where the true problem lies. As long as the focus remains on what, if anything, should or should not be done with the millions of illegal immigrants already here, in addition to the thousands more that continue to pour in on a weekly basis, the focus remains off the root causes of the problem; the companies that hire illegal labor, making our country a magnet that draws illegal immigrants across our borders in the same fashion that gravity forces falling objects to ground out of the sky, along with the politicians that refuse to secure the border and take action against companies utilizing illegal labor. If we are going to have a debate on illegal immigration in this country, let's have the full debate, not just debate the part controlled by the liberal agenda driven American media.

So who is really to blame for this problem? The illegal immigrants? Technically, yes. They know they are breaking our laws when they come to our country and ruin the job market, many times using false names and/or false social security numbers. Do I blame them for the problem? No, not really—or at least not completely. And I don't believe most Americans do either.

Truth be told, if I was on the other side of the border with a hungry family and saw how easy it was to stroll across the border and get a job, I would probably do the same thing. After all, they are receiving so many mixed messages. They know, technically, they are breaking the law, yet people here are not only willing, but often times anxious, to hire them, politicians blatantly defend them and protestors march in the streets in support of them. Not to mention, they can actually hire businesses (for lack of better word) to help them get across the border.

Remove the first group from this equation, however, and the others become irrelevant. And just to set the record straight, my assertions are not directed at all American businesses. On the contrary, I realize there are literally millions of outstanding American companies from international corporations all the way down to small mom and pop, family owned businesses that play by all the rules, pay well, value employee morale and longevity, and are nothing short of an honor and privilege to work for. As a matter of fact, I would put that first factory I worked for in that category. And I certainly feel the same way about the company I currently work for. Thankfully, the companies whom I decry are a very small minority in the overall picture in this country. But if these companies are allowed to continue to grow in number, while the good ones close up shop because they can no longer compete with the vastly lower operating costs, all bets are off.

Let's revisit that poultry plant. Conditions there were miserable. Virtually every work area in a production area of that plant was either far too hot or way too cold for comfort. The floors were always wet, many areas of the plant were littered with blood, guts, feathers, beaks and feet; and raw chicken—especially in mass quantity—stinks. There wasn't one realistic thing that company could have done to eliminate, or even reduce, any of those negative factors. They were all just part of what came along with that industry. And people need to realize that, going in, and understand that if they chose to go into this line of work, these are all things they will have to deal with on a daily basis.

Realizing they had what many people would consider one strike against them already, however, due to the undesirable working conditions, this company could have chosen to try to find ways to offer employees incentives in other areas. Instead, they chose to double down on the undesirability of their facility by paying people as little as they could get away with while adopting a barbaric, sweatshop style management philosophy that made employees hate the very company they worked for. Then they took it a step further by insulting employees with indoor outhouses and many times inaccessible restroom facilities, subjecting employees to unsafe working conditions, working people as hard and as long as they could until they were ready to fall down from exhaustion—without ever whispering so much as a thank-you, and firing people routinely, in many cases apparently just to intimidate the rest of the workforce and keep them on edge.

And when they couldn't find Americans willing to work under these near slave conditions, they imported people from suffering nations who were desperate enough to comply. These are the types of companies that will decimate the middle class, should they ever become the norm instead of the exception.

Yet, if you listen to the message constantly echoed in the media, the reason companies hire illegal Hispanics is that Americans are lazy, irresponsible, allergic to hard work and afraid to get their hands dirty. Well, as an American who is none of the above and has had the privilege of working side by side with hundreds, if not thousands, of other Americans who are also none of the above, I'm mad as hell and I'm not going to take it anymore!

Government officials have to clamp down once and for all—and this insane episode in our nation's history is over. Hit them where it hurts, right in the pocketbook. If they would give companies one very expensive warning fine the first time they are caught hiring illegals, they would take the profit right out of hiring illegal immigrants. Then watch how quickly these companies warm back up to the American employees they once shunned. And if they're caught a second time, shut them down. If they're not going to employ Americans, or at least people in America legally, why should they be allowed to operate in America? Once there are no longer jobs for illegal immigrants, there will be no reason for them to come. And if there are no illegal immigrants coming here looking for jobs, the politicians have no one to defend and the protesters have no one to support. Problem solved.

And yes, it could be just that easy. If the jobs dried up tomorrow, most illegal immigrants would head home immediately, on their own, and there would be no need to debate what to do about the problem. Unless, of course, our government gives them dozens of other reasons to stay like, welfare, food stamps, housing assistance, and free health care.

I would like to close on a lighter note. I have been a columnist for many years. And although my first columns addressed serious editorial topics, once I switched to entertainment, the true little jokester in me came spilling out. I had the idea for a great short column to help express my own personal frustration and that of many other hard-working Americans when our current administration filed a lawsuit against Arizona for attempting to do what the federal government refused to do, and passed a law to enforce current immigration law that the federal government was ignoring. I had nowhere to publish it at the time, so I will share with you the column that almost never was.

A [Mostly] True Story.

Most of this really happened.

It was a typical afternoon in small town Georgia. I was driving on a local two-lane highway famous for never having any traffic—probably because the road also didn't have any traffic lights or even stop signs. As I went on, I noticed brake lights starting to illuminate ahead. As I drew closer, I realized traffic was at a standstill in both directions. Upon further observation, I also realized both sides of the roads were lined with flashing red and blue lights. "Must be one heck of a wreck up there," I thought to myself.

As I slowly inched my way up the line of traffic, I noticed no apparent wreckage, but there were cars pulled off and parked on the shoulders in both directions with state troopers walking from car to car. I was directed into the line of parked cars on the shoulder. After sitting there wasting time for who knows how long, I saw a trooper finally approaching my vehicle. He motioned for me to roll down the window and demanded to see my driver's license, vehicle registration and proof of insurance.

I thought about it for a second, and then responded. "It sounds to me an awful lot like you're asking to see my papers. Our President says you can't do that."

"Oh, no," the trooper replied with a devilish ear-to-ear grin. "That's just for citizens of other countries who willingly and knowingly sneak over our borders illegally, then commit document fraud and many times identity theft, as well, to obtain illegal employment. As for you law-abiding citizens born in this country, we can delay, detain, inconvenience, poke, prod and harass you poor suckers all we want. As a matter of fact, I'm going to have to ask you to step out of the vehicle."

And all I was trying to do, during that trip, was take my child across town to get some ice cream.

ACKNOWLEDGEMENTS

This book would have never made it into its final, published form without the contributions from the following people that I would like to acknowledge and sincerely thank.

First and foremost I would like to thank my lovely wife, Laura, who contributed dozens of ideas and suggestions as well as devoted countless hours to proofreading before taking responsibility for final formatting. You are my best friend, companion, business partner, bookkeeper, proofreader and cheerleader. Your unwavering and unconditional support means far more to me than you'll ever realize.

To my daughter, Lindsey, who served as my second proofreader: I appreciate every page you've read and every suggestion you've made as well.

I'd also like to send a special thank you to my sister-in-law, Linda Thoma, for the awesome picture for the back cover.

Another special thank-you has to go to Martin DeMers of Algora Publishing for taking a chance on an Average Joe nobody-factory-worker and allowing me to tell a much-needed-to-hear story to an at least slightly-confused country.